stickyfaith

stickyfaith

youth worker edition

Practical ideas to
nurture long-term faith
in teenagers

Dr. Kara E. Powell
Brad M. Griffin &
Dr. Cheryl A. Crawford

 ZONDERVAN® youth specialties

ZONDERVAN.com/
AUTHORTRACKER
follow your favorite authors

ZONDERVAN

Sticky Faith, Youth Worker Edition
Copyright © 2011 by Kara E. Powell and Brad M. Griffin

YS Youth Specialties is a trademark of YOUTHWORKS!, INCORPORATED and is registered with the United States Patent and Trademark Office.

This title is also available as a Zondervan ebook. Visit www.zondervan.com/ebooks.

Requests for information should be addressed to:

Zondervan, *Grand Rapids, Michigan 49530*

Library of Congress Cataloging-in-Publication Data

Powell, Kara Eckmann, 1970-
    Sticky faith / by Kara E. Powell, Brad M. Griffin, and Cheryl A. Crawford. — Youth worker ed.
      p. cm.
      Includes bibliographical references and index.
      ISBN 978-0-310-88924-3 (softcover : alk. paper)
      1. Church work with youth. 2. Youth — Religious life. 3. College students — Religious life. I. Griffin, Brad M., 1976- II. Crawford, Cheryl A. III. Title.
    BV4447.P656 2011
    259'.23 — dc23   2011028203

Cover direction: Tammy Johnson
Cover photography: Reflex Stock
Interior design: Ben Fetterley and Matthew Van Zomeren

Printed in the United States of America

12 13 14 15 16 17 18 /DCI/ 22 21 20 19 18 17 16 15 14 13 12 11 10 9 8 7 6 5 4

To Nathan, Krista, and Jessica.
Your dad and I pray that you would always
know the Emmanuel, who sticks with us.
—*Kara E.*

To Anna, Kara, and Joel.
May you never forget the God who
can't stop loving you, no matter what.
—*Brad M.*

contents

acknowledgments

The insights found in these pages result from the collective work of a phenomenal team of researchers, youth leaders, and Fuller students over the six years of the College Transition Project. Special thanks to Dr. Cameron Lee for his steady consultation throughout this process, to Dr. Chloe Teller for keeping the team on track, to Dr. Chap Clark and Dr. Scott Cormode for their invaluable insights and contributions to the research, to Dr. Erika Knuth for crunching so many numbers, to Irene Cho for keeping the Fuller Youth Institute (FYI) running while we were preoccupied with this project, and especially to Dr. Krista Kubiak Crotty for asking the initial question that launched this whole adventure.

We'd also like to thank others who have served as part of the FYI staff and research team during this process, including Cody Charland, Nikki Chase, Emily Chen, Rana Choi Park, Marianne Croonquist, Kris Fernout, Mike Hensley, Dr. Andrea King, Melanie Lammers, Dr. Lydia Mariam, Meredith Miller, Paul Walker, and Matt Westbrook. A special heartfelt thanks to the Lilly Endowment for funding much of our Sticky Faith research.

We have been grateful for the 28 churches in our Sticky Faith Learning Cohorts who have served as incubators for this Sticky Faith movement: Bel Air Presbyterian (Los Angeles, CA), Calvary (Grand Rapids, MI), Christ Church of Oak Brook (Oak Brook, IL), Christ Community (Leawood, KS), Christ Presbyterian (Edina, MN), Due

West United Methodist (Marietta, GA), Evergreen Baptist (Los Angeles, CA), First United Methodist (Tulsa, OK), Frontline Community (Grand Rapids, MI), Grace Lutheran (Huntington Beach, CA), Green Bay Community (Green Bay, WI), Highland Park Presbyterian (Dallas, TX), Hillside Community (Rancho Cucamonga, CA), La Cañada Presbyterian (La Cañada, CA), Lake Avenue (Pasadena, CA), Mars Hill Bible (Grand Rapids, MI), Menlo Park Presbyterian (Menlo Park, CA), Meredith Drive Reformed (Des Moines, IA), Moraga Valley Presbyterian (Moraga, CA), Nampa First Nazarene (Nampa, ID), Newsong (Irvine, CA), Pasadena First Nazarene (Pasadena, CA), Peninsula Covenant (Redwood City, CA), Pulaski Heights United Methodist (Little Rock, AR), Richland Hills Church of Christ (Dallas, TX), Saratoga Federated (Saratoga, CA), Solana Beach Presbyterian (Solana Beach, CA), and Yuong Sang Church (Philadelphia, PA).

This book was made much better because of the input of wise friends and youth leaders who took the time to give us feedback, including Dave Powell and Missy Griffin (we wanted to mention them first), as well as Steve Argue, April Diaz, Dan Gannon, Mike Hensley, Megan Hutchinson, Johnny Johnston, Jeff Mattesich, Tim Nielson, and Jesse Oakes.

Your work has stuck with us and we are eager to see how the Lord builds even more Sticky Faith in kids.

1

the not-so-sticky faith reality

*I guess for a high school student I had an okay understanding
of my faith, but in college I was really forced to own the
values that I thought I had and make my own decisions . . .
I would definitely not say I've arrived by any means, but
I feel a lot of growth going on at this point.*
—Becca

*After Young Life and my youth group at church and
everything like that . . . I graduated and went off to
college, and I didn't hear back from those people again.
They didn't make any effort to stay in touch. So that
was kind of a disappointing experience.*
—Trevor

I (Kara) have two favorite professional football teams.

One is the San Diego Chargers. I'm from San Diego and have been following my beloved Chargers through their ups and downs for three decades.

My second-favorite team is whoever is playing the Oakland Raiders.

My love for football has been passed on to my son, Nathan. His top team is the San Diego Chargers ('atta boy!). His second-favorite team is the New Orleans Saints, a team he's rooted for since our family went to New Orleans after Hurricane Katrina to build homes for displaced families.

For Nathan's birthday a few years ago, we bought him a Chargers pennant and a Saints pennant. Being a Type-A mom, I suggested we tape his two new pennants to his bedroom wall that night. So Nathan and I put Scotch tape all over the back of the pennants and positioned the two flags on his wall right where we wanted them, staggered about 12 inches apart. They looked great.

For a few hours.

By the time Nathan woke up, both pennants were in a heap on the ground. The tape hadn't held.

Since the Scotch tape had failed, we decided to upgrade our tape selection. Before he went to bed that night, Nathan and I rummaged through our office supplies and found masking tape. Once again, we covered the back of each pennant with tape and hung them both up on the wall, hoping they would stay there.

The next morning, both pennants were still up. Nathan and I gave each other high-fives, excited that the masking tape had worked.

To our chagrin, when we got home that evening, both flags were back in that same dreaded heap on the ground.

So we pulled out the big guns. We grabbed our duct tape, plastered it across the back of the pennants, and for a third time hung both flags on Nathan's wall.

Both pennants were still hanging on the wall the next day. And the day after that. And the day after that. In fact, it's been over three years—and the duct tape has held. The pennants stuck.

Brad, Cheryl, and I wish we could say the same was true of the faith of teenagers in youth groups across the country—including the groups each of us works with. We wish we could say that the faith of these youth is so strong that even three years after high school graduation, they were still sticking with the Lord and with the church.

But we can't. To be honest, we've talked with countless high school graduates whose faith hasn't stuck three months, let alone three years.

The more that we at the Fuller Youth Institute study and talk with youth leaders and kids, the more we see that kids' faith is usually more like Scotch tape or masking tape. Maybe, just maybe, that faith is cohesive enough to hold them together through high school. Just barely. But then they graduate and tragically fall away.[1]

Tiffany's Story

From the first Sunday she walked into our high school ministry when she was in ninth grade, Tiffany plunged into every activity. She was deeply committed to knowing Jesus and making Jesus known. Any event we offered—youth choir, beach days, weekend service trips to Tijuana—Tiffany was there. Not only was she there, but she usually showed up at least 30 minutes early to see if she could help.

And help she did. She was especially good at making posters. She and I would spread paper across our youth room floor and try to come up with creative images to promote upcoming events or reinforce the teaching topic for the next week. When we made posters together, we talked about our mutual desire to know Jesus and help others know him too.

Around eleventh grade Tiffany started to change. She began to wear lots of dark, heavy makeup.

Her skirts grew shorter. A lot shorter.

She stopped arriving early for youth ministry events. She rarely signed up for anything. When I asked if she wanted to help with posters, she said she was too busy. Throughout Tiffany's senior year, her involvement at church grew more and more sporadic.

Six months after Tiffany graduated from high school, she became pregnant. She felt confused and ashamed—and wanted nothing to do with our church. Or me.

Her dad called me from the hospital the day Tiffany gave birth to her son. Although Tiffany had avoided me during her pregnancy, I asked her dad if she would be okay with me visiting her that day and meeting her son. She said yes.

When I walked into Tiffany's hospital room, I felt like the clock had been turned back three years. She had no makeup on and greeted me with a smile, clearly glad to see me. After we chatted for a few minutes, Tiffany offered to let me hold her son. It was the first time I'd ever held a baby who was only a few hours old. I told her so, and she grinned.

I asked Tiffany if I could pray for both her and her son, and she said yes. As I walked out of the hospital, I continued to pray—that the Lord would use this new son to somehow draw Tiffany back to her faith.

Any hope I had that Tiffany would reconnect with our church or with the Lord was shattered within weeks. I have no idea where she and her son are today.

I'm left with all sorts of questions: What happened to poster-making, attend-everything-our-youth-ministry-offered Tiffany? Why did her faith—a faith that seemed so vibrant at first—fail to stick? What could we have done differently that might have helped her develop a faith that would last?

Kids' Faith Isn't Sticking

If you are a youth leader, I'm guessing you have your own "Tiffanys." In fact, there are more "Tiffanys" than you may realize. The board of the National Association of Evangelicals, an umbrella group representing 60 denominations and dozens of ministries, has passed a resolution deploring "the epidemic of young people leaving the evangelical church."[2]

But is it really an "epidemic"? Does the data suggest that the number of youth group kids exiting from the faith is more like a trickle or a flood?

That's a tough question to answer, and one made more complicated by a few slippery terms. For example, what exactly is meant by a "youth group kid"? Is it a kid who is connected when he or she graduates from high school, or is it a kid who was connected at some point during high school? Unfortunately, a large percentage of kids don't stick with their faith throughout high school.

And how is "exiting from the faith" defined? If a college freshman doesn't go to church but prays before big exams, has she left the faith or not?

As we have examined other research, our conclusion is that 40 to 50 percent of kids who are connected to a youth group when they graduate high school will fail to stick with their faith in college.[3]

Let's translate that statistic to the kids in your youth ministry. Imagine the seniors in your youth ministry standing in a line and facing you. (I'm sure they are smiling adoringly at you, their beloved youth leader.) Now, imagine that you ask them to count off by twos, just like you used to do on the playground to divide into teams: "1 . . . 2 . . . 1 . . . 2 . . . 1 . . . 2 . . ." The 1s will stick with their faith; the 2s will shelve it.

> I think one thing [youth pastors] could have done is taught on sex more, I mean that's where I screwed up.
> —Clayton

As someone who's been working with teenagers in youth groups for almost 25 years, I'm not satisfied with a 50 percent rate of Sticky Faith.[4]

Are you?

I doubt it.

Here's another alarming statistic: Only 20 percent of college students who leave the church planned to do so during high school. The remaining 80 percent intended to stick with their faith—but didn't.[5]

As has been rightly pointed out, college is often a season of experimentation for teenagers who were raised in the church and are learning to truly own their faith. That hunch is in some ways supported by the encouraging statistic that somewhere between 30 and 60 percent of youth group graduates who abandon their faith and the church return to both in their late twenties.[6] Yet those young adults have already faced significant forks in the road regarding friendship, marriage, vocation, worldview, and lifestyle, all while their faith has been pushed to the backseat. They will have to live with the consequences of those decisions for the rest of their lives. Plus, while we can celebrate those who eventually place their faith back in the driver's seat, we still grieve over the 40 to 70 percent who won't.

College Students Gone Wild

From the movie *Animal House* to the Asher Roth song "I Love College," college life has been depicted as a nonstop merry-go-round of sex, drugs, and alcohol, with a few hours of study thrown in here and there. Granted, sex, drugs, and alcohol are not the ultimate litmus test of a college student's spirituality. (We'll say more about that in chapter 2). And of course, media portrayals of college kids are certainly exaggerated. Nonetheless, since more students are partying than we might realize, and since students' partying often affects their relationship with God, it's a factor we have to discuss as we consider what makes faith stick.

Each month, just less than 50 percent of full-time college students binge drink with alcohol, abuse prescription drugs, and/or abuse illegal drugs.[7] According to one analysis conducted by a professor of public health at Harvard University, the percentage of fraternity and sorority members who binge drink has climbed to 80 percent.[8]

This heavy alcohol consumption is costing students—a lot. According to one estimate, college students spend $5.5 billion each year on alcohol—more than they spend on soft drinks, tea, milk, juice, coffee, and schoolbooks combined.[9]

This widespread use of alcohol opens the door to the bedroom. Dr. Michael Kimmel, professor of sociology at State University of New York, has researched college behaviors extensively and has concluded, "Virtually all hooking up is lubricated with copious amounts of alcohol."[10]

As a youth worker, you've almost certainly heard the term *hooking up,* a phrase that refers to a variety of sexual behaviors, ranging from kissing to oral sex to intercourse, without any expectation of emotional commitment. College seniors average nearly seven hookups during their collegiate careers, with 28 percent of them hooking up ten times or more.[11]

Kimmel vividly captures the wild tone of college campuses today by explaining the effects on local health care:

Every single emergency room in every single hospital adjoining or near a college campus stocks extra supplies on Thursday nights—rape kits for the sexual assault victims, IV fluids for those who are dehydrated from alcohol-induced vomiting, and blood for drunk driving accidents.[12]

Christian Kids Gone Wild?

What about the kids who have spent their high school years in our youth groups? Are they as wild as the rest of college students?

The good news is that multiple studies indicate that students who are more religious and/or more likely to attend church or religious gatherings are less likely to consume alcohol or hook up.[13] Yet just because religious kids are *less likely* to party doesn't mean they aren't partying at all. In an exploratory pilot study we conducted early in our research, every single one of the 69 youth group graduates we surveyed drank alcohol during their first few years of college.

Cheryl focused her portion of our Sticky Faith research on youth group graduates who had been designated as "leaders" in their youth ministries in high school. Extensive conversations with these former student leaders revealed that loneliness and the search for friends seemed to push the buttons for everything else. The pri-

> I would walk about and see people do all kinds of stuff and then show up for a chapel service or a church service on Sunday, and I actually started calling them "weakened warriors" . . . it's a weird play on words because I spelled it w-e-a-k-e-n-e-d, like they are weakened people, but they are weekend warriors because they'd do all this stuff like these parties . . . and then I'd see them at church the next day and I'd be like, "Whoa, how you feeling man, 'cause you look like you drank three fifths of whiskey last night."
>
> —Andrew

mary reason students gave for participating in the party scene was because that's where "everyone" was. One student told her, "I don't think I've met many people who don't drink here. It's really hard to meet people if you don't drink." We found that students often made key decisions about involvement in these activities during the first two weeks of their freshman year.

The overall challenge of transitioning from high school to college was described well by one college senior we interviewed:

Transitioning out of high school into college is like you're leaving on a giant cruise ship. You're heading out of this harbor and everyone's waving you off. Let's say this ship is your faith. As soon as you start sailing out to this new port called college, you realize you're in a dingy. You don't have this huge ship, and you're completely not prepared, and your boat is sinking! Unless there's someone with a life raft who's ready to say, "We got you. Come right here. This is where you can be, and this is where you can grow," you're done.

Steps to Sticky Faith: Our Research

At the Fuller Youth Institute, we want to partner with you to offer kids a stronger "ship" of faith and extend a life raft to those who feel like they are already drowning. In all of our research initiatives, our mission is to leverage research into resources that elevate leaders, kids, and families. Thanks in large part to a sizable research grant from the Lilly Endowment, the Fuller Youth Institute launched the College Transition Project. Our six years of College Transition research from 2004–2010 have been fueled by two goals:

1. To better understand the dynamics of youth group graduates' transition to college; and
2. To pinpoint the steps youth workers, churches, parents, and students themselves can take to help students stay on the Sticky Faith path.[14]

Much of our passion for Sticky Faith grows from our own experience as youth leaders. I (Kara) have been in youth ministry for 24 years. In addition to my roles as the executive director of the Fuller Youth Institute and a faculty member at Fuller Seminary, I currently volunteer as a small group leader at Lake Avenue Church in Pasadena. Brad is younger (and, as I like to kid him, less mature) than I am, but in addition to his experience as the FYI associate director, he's logged more than 15 years in youth ministry and serves as a youth ministry and worship volunteer at his church. Cheryl tops us all with more than 30 years serving kids and college students in various capacities. Her PhD research at Fuller focused on an intensive interview study within the College Transition Project.

In our nearly 70 years of combined ministry experience, we've seen God build in students the kind of faith that is life changing—for them and those they impact. We're all in touch with students, from our various seasons of ministry, whose faith burns brighter than ever.

But then there are those whose faith has fizzled. We've all wondered for years what our youth ministries could have done better. We are grateful to the Lord that this research has given us some answers, which we in turn want to share with you.

Meet the Students We Studied

Over the last six years, the College Transition Project has evolved into a comprehensive study of more than 500 youth group graduates using a variety of established research methods. You'll hear more from these students through quotes in sidebars and at the start of each chapter. At the center of our research are two longitudinal studies that focused on a total of 384 youth group seniors during their first three years in college. In many ways, these students represent "typical" youth group seniors transitioning to college (i.e., they come from different regions across the United States; they attend a mix of public, private, and Christian colleges and vocational schools; and 59 percent are female and 41 percent are male). Yet in comparison to the typical student headed to college, the students in our sample tend to have higher high school grade point averages and are more likely to come from intact families. We also recruited students from churches that have full-time professional youth pastors, which means they are likely to come from larger than average youth groups (average youth group size is 50 to 75 students). From the outset, we want to admit that these factors bring a certain bias to our findings, a bias we diligently tried to counter by examining other research studies and by face-to-face interviews with students with more diverse academic, family, and church backgrounds.

In an effort to bring focus to our research, we recruited high school seniors who intended to enter college after graduation. For the purposes of our study, *college* includes studies at a four-year college or university, a junior college, or a vocational school. We can't be certain, but we think it's likely that our findings are also relevant to those entering the workforce or the military. Our hunch is supported by a parallel study indicating that church dropout rates for college students are not significantly different from the dropout rate for others from the same age group who do not attend college.[15]

Defining Sticky Faith

As we were initially conceptualizing our research project, we quickly ran into one important question: What exactly is Sticky Faith? While it's tempting to apply former U.S. Supreme Court Justice Potter Stuart's famous definition of obscenity ("I know it when I see it"), that doesn't fly in academic circles. Based on the research literature and our own understanding of students, we arrived at three characteristics of Sticky Faith; the first two are relevant for all ages, while the last has heightened importance during students' transition to college.

Sticky Faith is . . .

1. *Both internal and external:* Sticky Faith is part of a student's inner thoughts and emotions, and is also externalized in choices and actions that reflect this faith commitment. These behaviors include regular attendance in a church or campus group, prayer and Bible reading, service to others, and lower participation in risk behaviors, especially sex and alcohol. In other words, Sticky Faith involves whole-person life integration, at least to some degree.

2. *Both personal and communal:* Sticky Faith celebrates God's specific care for each person while always locating faith in the global and local community of the church.[16]

3. *Both mature and maturing:* Sticky Faith shows marks of spiritual maturity but is also in the process of growth. We don't assume a high school senior or college freshman (or a youth worker, for that matter) will have a completely "mature" faith. We are all in process.[17]

The vast majority of kids we interviewed—even those who had thrived in college—reported that college had been a time of both challenge and growth, a period full of new perspectives and experiences. Reading through the transcripts, it seems that the typical college student sits down at a table full of new and interesting worldviews and people. Instead of allowing faith to be merely one of many voices clamoring to be heard, those with Sticky Faith had determined their faith would sit at the head of the table.

> For more on the questions we asked in our College Transition Project, please see the Appendix as well as www.stickyfaith.org.

The Benefits of a Longitudinal Study

We designed our study to be longitudinal, meaning we followed youth group graduates over time, so we could track their individual and collective journeys during their first three years in college. The majority of the students we surveyed took their first online or paper questionnaire during the spring of their senior year in high school, and then one or two online questionnaires during their freshman, sophomore, and junior years in college. Each wave of data collection allowed us to peel away less significant layers of the transition so we could focus on what lay at the Sticky Faith core.[18]

Sticky Findings and Sticky Faith Made Practical

We have divided each chapter into two sections, the first of which is called **Sticky Findings**. In that first section, we summarize the most important things we've learned from our College Transition Project, from other parallel studies, as well as from our ongoing explorations of theology and Scripture. As researchers with a Practical Theology bent, we are convinced that simply crunching numbers about students' experiences and behaviors will leave us splashing around in the shallow end. It's when we pair our study of students with a thorough examination of theology and Scripture that we are able to dive into deeper waters.

The members of our College Transition Project research team have extensive backgrounds in youth ministry, enabling us to bridge the sometimes-wide chasm between empirical statistics and sound ministry programs. Our team's initial hunches about ministry implications were then tested and refined through one-on-one consultations with youth leaders, youth worker focus groups and summits, and nationwide seminars with youth pastors and volunteers.

A highlight of this iterative process was our yearlong Sticky Faith Learning Cohort. We invited 12 innovative churches from around the United States to apply our Sticky Faith research to their settings to offer more transformative youth and family ministry. Through two summits and monthly webinars, these churches became 12 diverse incubators for Sticky Faith ministry. My (Kara's) church was part of the group, giving me an up-close-and-personal view of the Sticky Faith process. The following year, we repeated this process with 16 more churches, for a total of 28 congregations whose stories are sprinkled throughout this book.

> If you're interested in learning more about how your church could participate in future Sticky Faith cohorts, please visit www.stickyfaith.org.

Based on the Sticky Faith Learning Cohorts and additional dialogue with other churches of various sizes, denominations, and geographical locations, we can recommend a robust list of proven and practical ministry ideas. Those ideas are described in detail in the second section of each chapter, labeled **Sticky Faith Made Practical.**

It's Never Too Early

Early in our research, we concluded that building Sticky Faith doesn't start when high school students are seniors, or even juniors. The reality is that students' faith trajectories are formed long before twelfth grade. Although we have devoted chapter 8 to the particular challenges of building Sticky Faith in high school seniors as they prepare for college, we encourage you to apply the rest of the book to all your high school students—and your middle school students, too. In fact, many of these findings have relevance for kids at even younger ages. My (Kara's) three children are eleven, nine, and five years old; Brad's three children are nine, six, and three; our research impacts the way we and our spouses parent every day.

You'll be more likely to develop Sticky Faith in students when you share our research with parents of kids of all ages, as well as senior adults who have an understandably soft spot for their own grandkids. Try to create as broad a Sticky Faith team as possible in your youth ministry or church (more on that in chapter 4). After studying seniors' transitions to college, Dr. Tim Clydesdale, a sociologist at the College of New Jersey, concluded, "Given the seeming importance of retaining youth for most religious groups in the United States, it is striking how haphazardly most congregations go about it."[19]

It's time to end the haphazard way we prepare kids for all they will face in the future.

It's time to get out the duct tape.

It's time to build Sticky Faith.

Above the Research:
A Loving and Faithful God

As much as we wish there were a foolproof plan for Sticky Faith, we will be the first to admit there isn't. There is no Sticky Faith silver bullet. There is no simple list of steps you can take to give youth a faith that lasts. Part of what makes youth ministry so demanding is that there are rarely easy answers.

That might be disappointing, but let us make a few additional admissions that we hope will encourage you.

- As much as we love research, we will also be the first to admit that we love God more.
- As much as we believe in research, we will also quickly admit that we believe in God more.
- As much we value sorting through data, we value prayer far, far more.

Whenever we share our research with youth leaders, including leaders who are grieving the way their own children have strayed from the Sticky Faith path, we are reminded of the God who transcends all research and all easy answers. We are struck by how much we need to depend on God for wisdom, strength, and miracles. After all, faith always involves a fair amount of mystery, hoping for things unseen (Hebrews 11:1). Ultimately, it is the Holy Spirit, not us, who develops Sticky Faith in kids.

As a result of our research, our nationwide conversations with kids and leaders, and even our ministry experience, we have learned much about Sticky Faith. We are full of suggestions. But our *top* suggestion is this: Trust the Lord with your kids and continue to ask—maybe at times beg—the Lord to build Sticky Faith.

sticky discussion questions

1. When people decide to read a book, they are often trying to solve a problem. What problem(s) are you hoping to address by reading this book?

2. How would *you* define "Sticky Faith"?

3. As you think about your youth ministry leadership up to now, what have you done that has helped your kids develop a long-term faith? What do you wish you had done differently?

4. What are the ramifications for your youth ministry if you follow the advice that it's "never too early" to start thinking about Sticky Faith?

5. Do you agree that the top suggestion for youth leaders should be to trust the Lord with kids and beg the Lord to build Sticky Faith? Perhaps you'd like to put this book down and pray for a few moments before you turn the page . . .

2

the sticky gospel

I wish the high school youth pastors would focus perhaps less on, you know, the Romans Road and the 8 steps to success for how to convert somebody . . . and more on living a life that other people are gonna want to live, because that's what's compelling and that's what's gonna bring people in. That's the best advertisement for God and for Christianity.
—Sara

I have no clear conception of God now—and I probably did in high school, although it's hard to construct the way that I thought then. I have begun to pull out of my crisis of faith—I think—and I am sure that God exists. But now my philosophical views very much tend towards irrationalism and a kind of nihilistic skepticism, so I have a lot of trouble coming to terms with Christianity. I am trying to believe, but I'm not sure whether I'll ever be able to do it again.
—Cy

Through studying and experiencing God, I have given up on trying to put God inside of a box, and I have given up on trying to attempt to explain all of the details about who he is. I am seeing that he is still a God who gets angry, still a God who demands justice, still the God of the oppressed, still the God of the downtrodden, still the God who loves all— regardless of their ethnicity. Basically, I have encountered the living and uncontrollable God who is in the Bible, not the wimpy passive God I learned about in Sunday school.
—Denise

The carpet suddenly looks so fascinating.

Or so it seems whenever I (Kara) ask youth leaders to describe the gospel to a roomful of their colleagues. As soon as I ask for volunteers willing to share their own descriptions of the gospel, heads bow and eyes look down at the carpet.

No, it's not because they are deep in prayer.

It's because they are desperately trying to avoid looking me in the eye, fearing that if no one volunteers, I might call upon them.

How do *you* define the gospel?

It's a question I ask every time I speak about Sticky Faith. In fact, I'll tell you what I tell the youth leaders in the audience: *When it comes to Sticky Faith, there is nothing more important than students' view of the gospel.*

The *gospel* is not an easy term to define. In fact, my first faculty meeting after I came to Fuller featured a panel of distinguished Fuller professors sharing their own descriptions of the gospel. Here were biblical scholars who had been studying Scripture longer than I'd been alive, and they were still wrestling with the meaning of the gospel.

Part of that wrestling is inevitable. If the gospel were easy to define, then it wouldn't be God-sized.

And yet as leaders—not to mention followers of Jesus—we need to keep wrestling with the meaning of the gospel until we pin down some answers. Our lack of clarity about the "good news" is mirrored—and magnified—in our students.

In reference to preachers, it's been rightly said that a mist in the pulpit often becomes a fog in the pew. The same is true—perhaps even more true—for those of us who teach and work with youth.

In this chapter, we hope to clear away the fog that has clouded our students'—and our own—view of the gospel. More than any other section of this book, this chapter is dripping with Scripture because we believe that Scripture—when properly and contextually understood and applied—is the ultimate authority on all topics, including the Sticky Gospel. As we teach and model for our kids the Sticky Gospel that is itself taught and modeled in Scripture, we have the best chance of discovering a relationship with Jesus that is vibrant and lasting.

Sticky Findings

Many of our kids—even those who grew up in church—have surprising views of what it means to be a Christian.

You might think that asking college juniors who are youth group alums to define what it means to "be a Christian" would be a pretty straightforward question. You would be wrong.

Of the 168 youth group graduates who answered our question, 35 percent gave an answer that didn't mention Jesus at all. Granted, two-thirds of those kids who didn't mention Jesus mentioned God, but the number of youth who define Christianity without any reference to Jesus remains disturbing.

The most dominant theme in youth group graduates' descriptions of being a Christian was that it meant to "love others." Certainly, that is a major theme of Jesus' teaching. In fact, Jesus declared that "Love your neighbor as yourself" was the second most important commandment (Matthew 22:39). But it comes after the first and greatest commandment, which is to "Love the Lord your God with all your heart and with all your soul and with all your mind" (Matthew 22:37).

Even most atheist teens think it's a good idea to love other people. And they are right. It is. But the type of Sticky Faith that lasts long-term demands a bigger, Jesus-centered view of the gospel.

It's ultimately students' internal faith—not their involvement in religious activities—that matters most.

As part of our research, we examined youth group kids' use of alcohol both before and after graduation. Now we are the first to admit that alcohol is not the ultimate litmus test of spiritual maturity or Sticky Faith. Sticky Faith is ultimately a heart issue and a matter of a student's internal trust in the Lord. Yet, as we'll explore later in this chapter, our inner love for the Lord will overflow through a kingdom lifestyle in all we do and are. Given how many youth group graduates are drinking alcohol, and how much they are drinking, their use and abuse of alcohol sheds light on some of their challenges in embracing and living out this inner commitment to Jesus.

When we surveyed college freshmen, we found a significant inverse relationship between students' alcohol consumption and their spiritual maturity. In other words, students who reported more internal signs of embracing their faith also drank less alcohol. That's what most of us would expect.

The same was *not* true of students' religious behaviors. A student's level of involvement in religious acts such as praying, reading the Bible, and attending worship services had no significant relationship with his or her alcohol consumption.

This data suggests that there seems to be a difference between a sticky, internalized faith and a faith based on religious practices.

Students seem to have embraced a "Red Bull" gospel.

The average youth group graduate drinks more alcohol in college than she did in high school. That shouldn't surprise you. You probably would have guessed that before you picked up this book. That finding in and of itself is not worth a major grant and six years of research.

But here's some data that is. We also looked at the rate of increase in alcohol use among different types of students. Guess which kids showed the greatest increase in drinking alcohol as they bridged from high school to college?

The teetotalers.[1]

Yes, it's the kid who didn't drink at all in high school who gets to college and comes undone.

We found a similar increase in sexual activity. Youth group graduates who reported no sexual activity in high school showed a significant increase in sexual activity as college freshmen. Our students who were sexually active in high school actually reported a drop in sexual activity in their first semester in college, with it rebounding to levels similar to high school by their second semester.[2]

Many of the kids who said yes and no at the right times during high school had what we at the Fuller Youth Institute call a "Red

Bull" view of the gospel. After all, Red Bull's sugar and caffeine (as well as some other ingredients I can't decipher) can get you through a few tough hours. But eventually you crash. And crash hard.

Similarly, our youth group kids often have a Red Bull experience of the gospel. This gospel is potent enough to help them make the right decision at a Friday night party in high school, but the Red Bull gospel and the support of other Red Bull gospel followers isn't powerful enough to foster long-term faith.

Many youth group kids have adopted the "gospel of sin management."

The kids who populate our youth groups often have an extremely superficial view of the gospel. They view the gospel like a jacket they can take on and off based on what they feel like doing that day. If they're going to church or hanging out with Christians, they put on their gospel jacket. If they're headed to a party or drifting toward spiritual apathy, they toss that gospel jacket into a corner.

Our kids can stuff the gospel into a corner for many reasons, one of which is that they have somehow picked up that living as a Christian means following a list of what they should and shouldn't do.

Do . . . go to church and youth group as often as possible, read your Bible, pray, give money, share your faith, get good grades, respect elders, spend spring break on a mission trip, and be a good kid.

Do not . . . watch the wrong movies, drink, do drugs, have sex, talk back, swear, hang out with the "wrong crowd," go to Cancun for spring break, or go to parties.

If students aren't good at following the "do" list, then this gospel isn't only unappealing, it's irrelevant.

Philosopher Dallas Willard coined a phrase that sums up this way of thinking. He called it the "gospel of sin management":

> *History has brought us to the point where the Christian message is thought to be essentially concerned with only how to deal with sin: with wrongdoing or wrong-being and its effects. Life, our actual existence, is not included in what is now presented as the heart of the*

*Christian message, or it is included only marginally . . . The current
gospel then becomes a "gospel of sin management."[3]*

Kids are not picking up this gospel of sin management in a vacuum. They are learning this gospel from us—from the gospel we believe, talk about, and, most important, model to them. Unfortunately, we've let the gospel deteriorate into a list of good virtues, and then we slap Bible verses on them. We've given our youth group kids a shrunken version of the gospel that fits inside the small box of "sin management." I don't blame them for tossing that gospel aside.

A central theme of Paul's gospel is freedom, and that includes freedom from the bondage of "good things."

This gospel of sin management couldn't be further from the gospel described by the apostle Paul in his epistles. One of Paul's most pointed and concise explanations of the gospel in practice is in Galatians, especially its fifth chapter.[4]

The first verse of Galatians 5 is considered by some to be the summative verse of all of Paul's writings: "It is for freedom that Christ has set us free. Stand firm, then, and do not let yourselves be burdened again by a yoke of slavery." In a surprising twist, the "slavery" Paul goes on to describe doesn't involve bondage to sinful behaviors as we and our students might expect (e.g., all those "don'ts" we talked about earlier). Ironically, Paul championed freedom from something that up until that time had been encouraged as a virtuous, even necessary, religious rite: circumcision.[5]

Among the questions about following Jesus in the midst of first-century traditions, a major rift over circumcision had crept into the church at Galatia, one so serious that it was damaging the fledgling Christian movement. On one side were faithful Jewish Christians whose understanding of faith in God through Christ was dependent upon their Jewish roots, history, and faith, especially male circumcision.

On the other side of the division were those who were not Jews, called Gentiles, who had come to faith in Christ. They struggled with the Jewish adherence to circumcision, mostly because it didn't seem to jive with the gospel they'd heard from Paul.

Paul jumps into the debate feet-first and aligns with the Gentile converts: "Mark my words! I, Paul, tell you that if you let yourselves be circumcised, Christ will be of no value to you at all. Again I declare to every man who lets himself be circumcised that he is obligated to obey the whole law. You who are trying to be justified by the law have been alienated from Christ; you have fallen away from grace" (Galatians 5:2-4).

Paul uses the rift in Galatia to demonstrate God's intent and plan for all people since the beginning: It is not anything *we do* that makes us pure enough to please and come close to a holy God, but it's what *God has done* and continues to do in and through us. Paul makes it clear there is no middle ground: Either you place your trust in Jesus as the Lord who saves and makes you righteous by his Spirit, or you trust in yourself, meaning your ability and commitment to live in obedience to the Law.[6]

This theme of freedom—including freedom from acts that at other times had been labeled as godly—can be somewhat counterintuitive to us. Many of us were taught a faith formula that said Christ has already done his job by dying for us; our job is to respond by living up to the behavioral expectations of the gospel. The concept of freedom can also cause a little anxiety when it comes to our youth ministries, because many of us have been taught, or at least modeled (usually unintentionally), that freedom doesn't actually mean *freedom*, but rather switching from one form of bondage (sin) to another (the gospel of "sin management").

The Sticky Faith Process of Galatians 5:5: Faith + Waiting on God → Righteousness

Paul describes our role in this Sticky Gospel in Galatians 5:5: "For through the Spirit we eagerly await by faith the righteousness for which we hope." In other words, it is God's job to work in us and to present us as righteous; our job is to learn to trust God and let the process proceed.

The Pharisee Gospel

God gave Israel the Law and the Prophets, what we call the Old Testament, to demonstrate the "righteousness" he intends for and from his people. But when humanity fell, we became powerless to fulfill the demands of the Law. As Paul says in Romans 3:23, "It is the straight-edge of the Law that shows us how crooked we are."[7]

When Jesus arrived, the demands of the Law were both satisfied and fulfilled in him, and a new process of righteousness through faith was put into place. In Christ's suffering, death, and resurrection, we are now given the free gift to trust God to make us righteous, by the presence and power of the Holy Spirit. The Old Testament, then, was and is a constant reminder that God's people cannot live up to who we were created to be without God changing us from the inside out, *not* the outside in.

For a biblical example of futile Law-based attempts at living from the outside-in, just look at the Pharisees, Jesus' biggest detractors during his time walking the earth. In Matthew 23, Jesus describes what an outside-in righteousness produces: "Woe to you, teachers of the law and Pharisees, you hypocrites! You are like whitewashed tombs, which look beautiful on the outside but on the inside are full of the bones of the dead and everything unclean. In the same way, on the outside you appear to people as righteous but on the inside you are full of hypocrisy and wickedness" (Matthew 23:27-28).

We may not say this outright, but it is so easy to slip into the kind of faith that says, "God loves you, sure . . . but God will *really* love you when you _____ (fill in the blank)." The Sticky Gospel of Galatians 5:5 means that instead of concentrating on whether or how our kids are living "righteous" lives, we youth leaders should focus on helping them discover and strengthen their trust and faith in Jesus Christ. In so doing, the righteousness they eventually display will be the product of the Holy Spirit.

Trusting this Sticky Faith process can be challenging. We tend to want outcomes that are immediate and measurable. Yet in life and in faith, growth is a process. The issue for us as we strive to help our kids embrace the Sticky Gospel is to realize that God is the one who will make them righteous as they trust him. Our job, then, is to help them learn to trust God and create the kind of environment in which they are able to explore faith and trust while practicing their freedom to respond in love. I'll be the first to admit this is easier said than done.

At the heart of the Sticky Gospel is the pursuit of trusting Christ. The good news is that Christ is already pursuing us.

This may sound obvious but I'll state it anyway: Faith is the key to the Sticky Gospel. In Galatians 5:5, the Greek word tranlated as "faith" is *pisteuo* (pronounced "pis-TAY-u-o"). This word is used throughout the New Testament and can be translated as three different but closely related words: *faith, believe,* or *trust.* So as a general rule, whenever we see the word *faith* or *believe* in the Bible, it generally comes from *pisteuo* and can also be translated as *trust.* In our work with kids, we have found that the concept of trusting God with a given issue, person, or circumstance is often easier to grasp than using the concepts of *faith* or *believe.* As you help your students understand Sticky Faith, then, every decision, every thought, and every action comes down to this: Where do I place my trust? Do I trust my own instincts, desires, and convictions, or do I trust Christ?

Jesus affirmed this as the key question when he was asked, "What must we do to do the works God requires?" Jesus answered, "The work of God is this: to believe (*pisteuo*) in the one he has sent" (John 6:28-29). Trusting in Christ is the primary calling God has for our kids—and for us—as we develop our faith.

Everything we do to grow spiritually is about trusting— even spiritual "disciplines."

In contrast with assuming it's our "work" that gives us deeper faith, the Sticky Faith process described by Paul shows that the way we deepen our trust is by putting ourselves in a position to draw close to God, even while the Holy Spirit is pursuing and surrounding us. This is the function of "spiritual disciplines." Disciplines do not make us righteous because we do them; instead, they put us in a position to be drawn into trusting Christ more fully.

Paul's insight that "in Christ Jesus neither circumcision nor uncircumcision has any value" (Galatians 5:6) is not limited to circumcision or other ancient Hebrew rituals. It also applies to our contemporary attempts to climb the ladder of righteousness through our own self-imposed gospel of sin management. We can insert any of today's devotional duties that we say are the essence of faith into Paul's phrasing: "In Christ Jesus," for example, "neither reading the Bible nor not reading the Bible has any value . . ." *in and of itself!*

If we are reading Scripture because we think our studying will make us more righteous, we are in effect saying we don't need God to change us because we can and do change ourselves. In contrast, the Sticky Gospel reminds us that our focus is to trust, and God promises to work within us at every stage of the process—by strengthening our trust, by giving us peace and patience as we wait for our lives to be transformed, and by actually changing us from the inside out.

The theme of focusing first on internal transformation instead of external behaviors is echoed by Paul in Philippians 3:1-14. Paul calls his circumcision and his zealous pursuit of righteousness based on the law "garbage" when compared with knowing Christ. In Philippians 3:12, Paul writes that he will "press on to take hold of that for which Christ Jesus took hold of me."

Sticky Faith in teenagers is not about "doing," it's about "trusting."

When we teach a faith that focuses on doing "the right things," kids may feel they can sustain this performance style of Christianity (often motivated by a desire to please adults). This faith based on how well they "live" the gospel may sustain them . . . for a season.

But this gospel of sin management can only last so long. Almost inevitably, when kids reach the awareness—through failure, pain, insecurity, or inner wrestling—that they do not have the power, capacity, and (often) interest in keeping the faith treadmill going, they will become either discouraged or complacent and put their faith aside.

To help our kids discover and grab hold of a sustainable, long-term, and vibrant Sticky Faith, we must stay true to the words of Jesus and heed the counsel of Paul: Trust in the one the Father has sent and live convinced that the only thing that counts is faith expressing itself through love.

Sticky Faith Made Practical

These insights from Galatians about the gospel of freedom have been some of God's most important lessons for me (Kara) personally in the last few years. Two years ago I meditated on Galatians 5:1-6 for over a month—until I had it memorized. More than mere research insights, this Sticky Gospel of trust has ruined much of my own good-works orientation and replaced it with a greater appreciation for God's grace and freedom.

Now I want it to do the same for you and your students.

Teaching That Builds Sticky Faith

With a bit of thoughtful preparation, you can create space for the Holy Spirit to deepen your students' love for the Sticky Gospel every time you teach.

Explain your terms.

At one of our Sticky Faith Summits at Fuller, Jim Candy, pastor of family life ministries at Menlo Park Presbyterian Church, shared his belief that using "Christianese" or theological terms around our youth without explaining their meanings is dangerous. Based on our research, we believe he's right.

When students hear you talk about the "Lamb of God" or "sanctification" (both biblical terms) but don't know what those words mean, students conclude that either they are stupid or the Christian faith is incomprehensible. If being at your youth ministry makes students feel stupid, they won't stay around for long. (Would you?) If they conclude Christianity is over their heads, they'll be less likely to engage in personal study and ownership of their beliefs—key steps on the path to Sticky Faith.

One night after youth group, Jim debriefed the meeting with his adult leadership team and worship interns. That night they had led their students in a worship song that proclaimed "Hosannah" multiple times. Jim wondered aloud with his adult leaders if the youth knew what this word meant. Every adult said they were sure their students knew its definition.

Then Jim asked those same adults to explain what "Hosannah" meant. None of them could do it.

The moral to that story is pretty clear: Encouraging Sticky Faith means explaining to your students—and adults, for that matter—the meaning of important theological terms.

Teach with an understanding of the context of Scripture's imperatives.

In the midst of my search to understand the gospel, I read through all of Paul's epistles in one sitting, looking for connections between all God has done for us and all God wants us to do to show our trust in him. It was a great exercise—one I highly recommend you try at home.

Interestingly, Paul's epistles by and large follow a pattern of starting with all God has done for us and then ending with the imperatives—the commands—of what we are to do in return. Let's look at Ephesians for example. In Ephesians 2:8, Paul famously proclaims, "For it is by grace you have been saved through faith—and this is not from yourselves, it is the gift of God." And yes, the word translated "faith" in the verse is *pisteuo,* so we can easily think of it as "trust." It is this trustworthy grace explained in the early chapters of the letter that allows us to live out Paul's commands to Ephesus in its final chapters, such as honoring our parents (6:2) and putting on the full armor of God (6:11).

Reformation scholar Michael Horton describes this progression as moving from the "indicative" to the "imperative."[8] In grammar, the indicative mood describes a state of being; in the case of Paul's letters, it often occurs in the earlier chapters when Paul describes who we are in Christ.

> God is not the friend he was in high school. He is now more like the grandparent in the home that I only visit on holidays or special occasions.
>
> —Ely

Having established who we are in Christ, we are then able to move into the "imperative" mood—meaning verb tenses that carry a sense of command.

When we teach, we often gravitate to texts at the end of Paul's letters—to those meaty commands we want youth to follow. The problem with starting there is that it's not where Paul started. Paul wanted his readers (both individually and corporately) to marinate in the power of trusting in God before calling them to fiery obedience.

Last year our youth ministry was teaching a series on Ephesians. I volunteered to teach the Sunday morning lesson on Ephesians 5:21-33, Paul's now controversial passage about submission to one another in marriage. The other leaders seemed pretty pleased I had volunteered. No one else was exactly begging to teach that particular passage.

At the start of my lesson, I walked students through Ephesians 2:1-10, pointing out that all of our life, as well as any impetus we have to obey God, flows from our acceptance of God's grace and our resultant trust. This trust in God's grace fuels our obedience and motivates our lives to be great big thank-you notes in response to all God has already done for us.

That morning I did tackle Paul's teaching on submission (a topic beyond the scope of this book, but one that is "sticky" nonetheless!). But not before I felt confident that students understood Ephesians 2 as its precursor.

When you teach, how do you frame your invitations to obey God's commands? When your teenagers hear your talk, will they think they are supposed to obey God because God said so? Or will they understand that their obedience flows out of their trust in God and the Holy Spirit's work in and through them? Ask yourself these questions as you prepare your next lesson. In fact, ask yourself these questions as you prepare every lesson from now on.

Engage youth in case studies that help them figure out what it means to trust God.

More and more colleges and graduate schools are adopting case studies as a central tool to help students learn and apply their new insights. And for good reason. Case studies help students vicariously live out the principles you're discussing by applying them to situations they are likely to face.

In order to help students grasp what it means to trust God, create case studies set in school, home, or social situations.[9] While they can be about any topic, the most interesting case studies are those involving a complex scenario, such as how to respond to a friend who is unsure about his sexual orientation, what friendships with nonbelievers should look like, or whether or not it's okay to go to a party with alcohol if you don't drink. Regardless of the plotline, invite students to discuss a few key questions:

- What would it look like to trust God in this situation?
- If you were trusting God, what would you do?
- What would you say?
- How would you explain your trust in God to others involved?
- What would it look like to doubt God in this situation? Is that bad?
- What do you suppose God would say to you about this? What might God's perspective be?

It's hard to tell you how my view on God has changed since I can't even tell if he's real or not anymore. Such devastation. Such heartbreak. I struggle to see how this can be real. I love my girlfriend more than I can even say. Words simply fail. I simply can't articulate how I feel about her. It's so powerful, so mind-blowing. It's amazing. Then I read that there is no love stronger than God's? So he is supposed to love me more than I could ever love her? That's incredible, because I would die to protect her. I would sacrifice ANYTHING for her happiness. There is nothing I wouldn't give her or do to prevent her from hurting. If God's love is stronger, then where has he been for the last three years? My best friend is dead. I was diagnosed with a disease I'll have until I die. My parents are scrambling to provide for their children. They call ME and cry. I lost my full-ride scholarship because someone thought it would be funny to pretend to be me and make fun of a college administrator . . . If I were that powerful, I wouldn't let even one of these things happen to her, or to anyone I love. If all that can happen and things just continually get worse . . . ? Some love.

—Gary

Expose students to real-life examples of others learning to trust God.

In a similar vein, invite parents and college students to share how they are learning to trust God in the everyday. Perhaps host a parent panel or invite individual parents to share their testimonies or faith journeys with your group, and then do the same with former group members who are now in college.

Contrast "Good Things Christians Do" with "Trusting in a Good God."

Consider starting one of your lessons by asking each student to make a list of 10 things he or she does to live like a Christian. Invite each student to offer a few responses and then see if anyone is willing to share how they feel as they hear everyone's lists. Odds are good that it will feel overwhelming—because it is. Contrast that long list with the freedom and trust Paul describes in Galatians 5, then give students a chance to share areas in which they want to more radically trust in God. If you have a flair for the dramatic, invite students to rip up their lists of "things they try to do" and instead have them simply write on a sheet of paper: Trust God.

For additional creative teaching ideas to help your students understand the Sticky Gospel and Sticky Faith overall, check out the *Sticky Faith Curriculum* available at www.stickyfaith.org.

Make trust an ongoing theme of your teaching.

Even Jesus had to repeat things over and over . . . and over . . . and over. So in the midst of your teaching topics, dream with students about what it means to trust God.

- When you're teaching about money, ask: What does it look like to trust God and give lavishly to the child our ministry has adopted through Compassion International or World Vision?
- When you're inviting students to go to Guatemala for a weeklong summer mission trip, ask: What does it look like to trust God with your time and the money you were hoping to earn that week at your job?
- When you're talking about social networking, ask: What does it look like to trust God with the number and type of folks you "friend"?
- When you're discussing partying, ask: What does it look like to trust God with your weekend plans, as well as your friendships, when it seems like "everyone" is going to that Friday night party that is bound to get out of control?

Unlock students' imaginations and dreams about trust. You'll likely end up surprised by their creativity and their courage.

Teach about recovery and repentance.

Your students—either during their time in your group or after they graduate—are going to mess up. They will make choices they regret and commit sins that surprise even them. The question is not "if" they will blow it, but "when."

When youth (or adults, for that matter) live by the "gospel of sin management," their faith isn't large enough to handle those inevitable mistakes. They've blown it. No Sticky Gospel here. They might as well toss in the towel. As a result, they often run away from both God and faith community at a time when they desperately need both.

The gospel of trust is big enough to handle sin. Your job is to help students know that. Your role as their teacher is to let them know ahead of time that if Jesus can't handle a little partying, we all need a new Jesus.

As a way of helping students understand that the love of Jesus is bigger than any sin we commit, one youth ministry hung a large board on their youth room wall with the phrase "Nothing can separate you from the love of God . . . Romans 8" plastered across the top. Using different pieces of torn construction paper, students were invited to anonymously write down whatever they wanted. What emerged were confessions, hurts, resentments, failures, and questions. Throughout the weeks that board remained on the wall, their youth pastor would periodically refer to "the board" as a place to start writing, and she also encouraged students to share what they wrote with one of the youth leaders.

Before students graduate from your group (and probably repeatedly during their time in your youth group), use this or another creative method to give students a healthy view of repentance through which they understand that their sins drive them closer to God instead of further away from God. Invite students to identify safe people and safe places to share their struggles so they can find a haven of love and understanding when they fall. Share some of your own struggles (in developmentally appropriate ways, of course— meaning you don't emotionally vomit all over your kids) so your students gain a snapshot of what it means to confess one's sin before others. Finally, offer yourself as someone your youth can turn to when their lives turn upside down. While none of us *loves* to get a call from a kid in crisis, we need to let youth know that we're willing to be that kind of safe place if one of them hits bottom.

Your Teachable Moments

The average student will learn more about Jesus from the way you greet her when she walks into your youth room and then listen— really listen—as she describes her day, than she will from your wonderful talk about Jesus at the end of the night. The typical youth group kid will take seriously your invitation to serve the poor when he sees you stopping after lunch to help someone who is homeless and begging on the street corner. These never-ending teachable moments you have with students form the informal—but usually more powerful—Sticky Gospel curriculum.

In your conversations with kids, focus on "Trusting God" before "Obeying God."

Theologically, "trust" and "obey" are not meant to be two separate-but-equal tasks of the Christian life. The two are intimately connected. *Trusting God* is the call of the gospel, as we've seen from Galatians 5. *Obedience* is our response as we trust.

How do you help youth understand that obeying God is rooted in trusting God? Imagine that Lecia tells you over coffee that someone in her English class keeps gossiping about her. Our default counseling style might be to offer a quick fix by tossing out a "bumper sticker" platitude and perhaps quoting a text like 2 Timothy 2:24: "And the Lord's servant must not be quarrelsome but must be kind to everyone." Then we might follow up with, "Lecia, God calls us to turn the other cheek and be kind to our enemies, even when it's hard." Done.

44

End of story. And it's true in as far as it goes. But maybe that's not the best approach if our goal is to help Lecia develop a Sticky Faith.

An alternative approach would be to use this hurtful gossip as a time to reinforce in Lecia what it means to trust Christ in ordinary life circumstances. First, ask her something like, "Where do you think Jesus is in the situation?" Depending on her answer, assure her that the Lord understands what she is going through and has been there. Following that, ask, "What do you think it might mean to trust Christ in the midst of this conflict?" Remind her that Christ can be trusted even when others cannot and that the Lord has promised to be with her and protect her. Then, as you talk about trusting God who is faithful and powerful, she will be empowered to respond to the one who has hurt her.

Instead of offering quick and directive advice, take the time to help your students respond to their circumstances from the standpoint of trusting. An emphasis on learning to trust points youth to an obedience based on walking with God, as opposed to "Be nice, because God says so."

Get past "Sunday school answers."

If you're talking with a student and you can tell he's giving you the answers he thinks you want to hear, push him a bit deeper by asking, "Why?" or "What makes you say that?" It's tempting to ignore the nagging inner voice that sometimes tells us our students are simply repeating "Sunday school" answers. Perhaps we do so because we're too busy or because we sincerely hope our kids actually believe those pat answers. But pay attention to that inner voice and take the time to dig a bit deeper in your conversations to unearth the true treasure of hearing students' authentic thoughts and feelings. As one youth worker in our Sticky Faith Learning Cohort advised, "Playing devil's advocate with your students can actually build their faith."

Express your trust and belief in your students.

Earlier in this chapter, we talked about the importance of teaching students that the Sticky Gospel is big enough to handle their struggles and sins. Every time you interact with students who have blown it, you have a teachable moment to model your trust and belief in them and in the God who is still working in them and through them.

One youth worker friend of mine, Roberto, learned this firsthand from a 2 a.m. phone call from one of his students. When you're a youth leader, 2 a.m. phone calls from students are never good.

This one was no exception. On the other end of the line was one of Roberto's students who quickly confessed, "I just slept with my girlfriend." The young man's girlfriend was also part of the youth ministry.

Roberto's heart started pounding as he offered to meet with the student for breakfast that morning.

For the rest of the night, Roberto did what you would have done, which was pray a lot and sleep only a little. When Roberto showed up for breakfast, the kid was already sitting at the restaurant table. Roberto started to express how much he loved him, and that God loved him, and that it was God's kindness that leads us to repentance. (See Romans 2:4.)

The high school kid stopped Roberto before he got much further, "Actually, I didn't sleep with my girlfriend. I just wanted to see how you would respond to me if I had."

Now, *that* kid needs therapy.

But I would guess that most—and maybe all—of our students are in more subtle ways wondering if we can *really* handle their failures. Every time our students share their struggles with us, we have the opportunity to pair their need to confess their sins with the freedom that comes from trusting God. It's all the better when that confession and freedom is wrapped in a blanket of our own verbal affirmation of God's never-stopping love.

More Caught Than Taught

When the students in our survey were college seniors, we asked them how participation in their high school youth groups had shaped them—both then and now. Youth group activities were rarely mentioned. Youth group talks were mentioned even less frequently.

What *was* mentioned was the legacy of youth leaders—a legacy derived not from what the leaders said or even what they did, but more from who they were. As one senior with a thriving faith four years out of youth group recalled about her youth leaders, "They were really good Christian role models and . . . the relationships they had with God kinda showed me the relationship I could have with him."

Your own love for the Sticky Gospel of trusting God will be more caught than taught. Students emulate better than they listen. As you live out your trust-centered faith, your life will never be static, stale, or boring. You will be disappointed, discouraged, and maybe even thrown around a bit at times. You likely will even wonder if such a life is really worth it. But as you faithfully hold on to the God who has taken hold of you, the life you live and model will be a beacon of hope and direction that no "sin management gospel" can hope to achieve. As you trust the gospel and the Lord who saves, your love of the Sticky Gospel will help your students fall in love with Jesus also.

sticky discussion questions

1. How would you have defined the gospel before reading this chapter? How about now?

2. Dallas Willard describes the "gospel of sin management" as only dealing with sin and its effects, instead of the ultimate freedom and grace we experience in Christ. In what way(s) is your faith an experience of the "gospel of sin management"?

3. How do you see your students' faith in light of this chapter? Where do you see them growing in what it means to trust Christ, and where do you see them living out of the "do's and don'ts" of Christianity?

4. When you teach, how do you frame your invitations to students to obey God's commands? Ask yourself: If I were a teenager hearing this talk, would I think I was supposed to obey God because God said so? Or would I know that my obedience flowed out of my trust and the Holy Spirit's work in and through me?

5. How can you better take advantage of teachable moments this week to help students see the Sticky Gospel?

6. In light of what you've just read, how would you like to respond when one of your students shares with you about a sin he or she has committed?

3

sticky identity

*I heard someone say "the fence is down," and by that
they meant the fence of your school, your family, your church,
your friends, who were once a fence around you, saying, "This
is the type of person that you are," or "This is what you are
and are not allowed to do," or "This is what is and is not
appropriate." That fence drops way down as soon as you get to
college, and I saw that instantly. First day on campus, your parents drive away, no one knows you . . . Suddenly I was faced
with this situation in which I literally could have re-created
myself in some ways if I wanted to, and nobody would
have known that I had ever been any different.*
—Emily

*When I started college, I was the person that my parents
wanted me to be. Now I feel like I found myself.*
—Max

A Tale of Two Freshmen

Katie launched with a bang into her freshman year at a large public
university.

Julia quietly and uneventfully entered a well-known private college in the Northeast.

Although Katie didn't like her roommate much, she found lots of fun and friendship by hanging out with other young women from her dorm floor. Julia bonded quickly with her Christian roommate and spent most of her free time with her.

For Katie, the partying began Wednesday night and didn't end until the wee hours of Monday morning. Drinking five or six beers and smoking pot became a mainstay of Katie's daily regimen.

Julia was shocked by the pervasiveness of alcohol at her school, but she eventually decided, along with her roommate, to drink a maximum of one drink per party so they could hang out with their new dorm friends.

Katie decided not to look into the Christian fellowship groups or a local church because she didn't have time, and a friend told her that the fellowship group on campus was cliquey. In her words, she decided to put her faith "on the shelf." Maybe after college she'll think about God once again. She has felt somewhat empty, but hasn't found her way back to God—just yet.

Julia immediately got involved in a campus fellowship group and local church, and describes her faith as challenged but growing.

Two girls who grew up in youth groups—youth groups probably not all that different than yours. Two very different life stories—with two very different faith trajectories. Although it is difficult to point out the definitive difference between Katie and Julia, a theme for them— and for countless others who are opting whether or not to stick with their faith—is their emerging identities.

Sticky Findings

DNA + Family + Social Environments ≠ Identity

At the Fuller Youth Institute our research with adolescents as they transition from high school to college has demonstrated the complexity of identity development. By *identity development,* we mean the process of figuring out who God has created us to be. Identity development is not formulaic by any stretch of the imagination. It's an intricate dance involving *all* of who your students are and their experiences—what researchers call "nature" and "nurture."

By "nature" we mean the physical components that impact kids' identities—both how they look (eye color, hair, height, weight) and less visible aspects, such as those hidden away in their genetic makeup or DNA.[1]

On the flip side are those aspects of identity that are largely driven by "nurture." Family background (including parents, siblings, extended family members, and cultural heritage) is one of the critical determinants of who your students will become, largely because of the amount of time they spend with their families. The social environment kids grow up in (their hometowns, schools, and neighborhoods) is another element of "nurture" that shapes who they become. I (Cheryl) grew up on a cul-de-sac in a Boston suburb where almost every household included six or seven kids. Because our neighborhood housed so many kids and the cul-de-sac provided a great "playing field," we gathered every day after school to play baseball, football, kickball, kick the can, or whatever other game we could dream up. This experience instilled in me a love for participating in sports and games that lasts to this day.

Largely because of the influence of social environments, a student's identity is both personal ("Who am I?") and communal ("Who am I as a part of us?"). This means the kids in your youth group are trying to figure out not only who they are as unique individuals, but also who they are as part of a larger community.

But in the midst of this interplay between "nature" and "nurture," there is still a gap. Who your youth group kids will become cannot be calculated by just adding up their DNA, their family backgrounds, and their social environments.

Enter God.

Although spiritual development is deeply connected to identity development, it is less understood and more mysterious.

The way God works in each individual is unique and immeasurable. That is not to say that God's work is "random" or capricious.

Rather, God's relationship with each of your students is as unique as the relationships those individuals have with their families and friends. Even among youth with similar backgrounds, God's relationship with each student is unique because God works in each of their lives in particular ways.

God's sovereign work in identity development was certainly apparent in one college freshman I interviewed. Esther was so over-the-top excited about God in her life, it took twice as many digital bytes for my recorder to capture all that she wanted to share. And yet, during her high school years, her parents dealt with alcoholism and depression—to the point where they were on the brink of divorce during Esther's junior year.

Esther spoke candidly of her conversations with each parent concerning their problems, which she then prayed about for hours on end. She recalled, "All of a sudden, things were working out, and God (and church) became the biggest part—the center—of our family life." Esther easily could have turned bitter toward God and her parents through this experience. Rather, she turned toward both—and continues to stick with both.

Even after all of our research and interviews with transitioning youth group kids, we still can't prescribe a foolproof fixed agenda to help all students grow in their spiritual identities or know who they are becoming in their journey with Christ. God's work in each life can neither be programmed nor predicted.

Our students' changing relationships mean the identity formation process lasts longer.

The timetable of youth identity development has shifted dramatically over the past few decades. During the 1960s, developmental psychologist Erik Erikson proposed eight stages of psychosocial development.[2] Erikson taught that adolescence was the time when kids figured out who they were—their identity. If this process didn't happen in kids, Erikson labeled them as "identity role-confused," which could lead to relational isolation later in their twenties.

Trust vs. Mistrust	Infancy (1 yr)	Do I trust my caretaker?
Autonomy vs. Shame & Doubt	Toddlerhood (1-3 yrs)	Do I feel secure enough to exert some independence?
Initiative vs. Guilt	Early Childhood (3-5 yrs)	Am I able to begin to take responsibility for myself?
Industry vs. Inferiority	Middle and Late Childhood (6-11yrs)	Am I mastering knowledge and skills?
Identity vs. Identity Confusion	Adolescence (11-25 yrs)	Am I exploring options and working toward commitment to who I want to be?
Intimacy vs. Isolation	Early Adulthood (25-40 yrs)	Am I closely connected to others? Or another?
Generativity vs. Stagnation	Middle Adulthood (40-60 yrs)	Am I helping prepare the next generation?
Integrity vs. Despair	Late Adulthood (60s +)	Life review: Have I accomplished anything during my life?

Five decades after Erikson made this claim, kids' social networks have grown to include "friends" they've never met—except online through Facebook, Myspace, or whatever emerging social network they will use next. Many of your ministry's adolescents maintain "membership" in several different peer crowds, allowing for inconsistent feedback as their identities form. A student who drops the F-bomb during football practice will receive a different reaction than if he did it during a church prayer retreat. Different contexts . . . different people . . . different responses.

Previous generations have often benefited from having their same friends attend their schools, churches, sports teams, and just about everything else. The feedback an individual received from friends was consistent across these multiple social contexts. Today's kids are more likely to interact with different friends in a variety of settings, which means they encounter a wider range of reactions to their words and actions. Plus, the ease of transportation has opened up more circles of relationships for students. Some kids travel miles with their friends on advanced sports teams to play similar athletes from other states or regions, while others get involved in regional orchestras, bands, or dance teams. Some of those same kids might attend a regional church, where families commute an hour away from home and community. The result of all of this driving is that kids (and adults) live very segmented lives, where their friends rarely overlap from context to context.

The breadth of peer relationships that young people experience means they get a wider variety of feedback about how they are perceived. Because friends' opinions matter so much during adolescence, the result is a delay in identity formation. Quite simply, kids receive *inconsistent* and *too much* feedback in response to what they say and how they act, so they often postpone committing to who they want to become.

Added to this is the fact that our cultural de-emphasis on families and communities has led many adolescents to struggle longer with identity issues. Our colleague Chap Clark concluded through his research that today's kids feel "abandoned" by adults.[3] During what may be the most difficult and confusing time of their lives, adolescents feel alone as they try to sort out who they are without the support or safety net of parents and other invested adults. In the absence of an adult safety net, they rely on the support system they've been forced to create: their "tribe" of friends.

During adolescence, kids need consistency and security as they "try on" different aspects of who they are, attempting to figure themselves out. The students we've studied say they're not getting the support they need. The result is that most of today's adolescents postpone the task of identity development until college—or beyond.

The reality is that most of them don't know what they want to do with their lives, and many of them *don't really care*. They want to enjoy college life; they will deal with who they are and what they will do with the rest of their lives later.

The freshman year of college: junior high do-over?

Every student I interviewed during the spring semester of their freshman year at college talked openly and courageously about the loneliness of that first fall semester. The depth of their longing for significant friendship was palpable. The reality is that most of these students had left towns, churches, and high schools where they knew others well and were known well. They lost lifelong buddies when they went off to college—or at least they lost daily, face-to-face contact with those friends. So they arrived at college with a profound need to be part of a group of friends.

The college freshman's need to belong looks a lot like the experience of students entering junior high.[4] Insecurity runs deep, so they anxiously look for friends who will like and accept them—or just hang out with them. Most college freshmen who live in campus housing find friends on their dorm floor—friends who, like them, are feeling the pangs of loneliness and the desire to be part of a crowd.[5] They often follow these new acquaintances to the nearest or "hottest" party, more because they are so desperate for friends than because they really want to party.

In fact, the most troubling aspect of youth group graduates' quest to overcome loneliness was *how* they tried to become part of a new group of friends. Every freshman I interviewed talked at length about the pervasive party scene—with alcohol as the focal point of the scene. Interestingly, they weren't drinking to get drunk. Instead, they were drinking to find friends. In other words, these freshmen were going to the parties simply to be accepted and begin to develop a group of friends. It was like junior high all over again—except with higher stakes.

Each adolescent's sense of identity proceeds through stages, yet sometimes those stages are not straightforward.

According to psychologist James Marcia, adolescents progress through four possible stages in their identity development, based on two criteria: *exploration* and *commitment. Exploration* occurs when your students seriously look at life options, such as faith, career, and the choice of a lifelong partner. When your students make definitive choices and move in a specific life direction, they are making *commitments.*

These four identity statuses are:

1. *Identity diffusion* occurs when an adolescent is unable or unwilling to explore or commit to any particular identity.[6]
2. *Foreclosure* occurs when an adolescent embraces clear commitments, but they're really the commitments of his or her parents or culture, chosen without exploring options.
3. *Moratorium* (sometimes referred to as "crisis") is a time of exploring options of who a student wants to be.
4. *Achievement* occurs when a student resolves the explorations of moratorium by making clear commitments.

Here's one way to visualize this theory, based on axes of crisis/no crisis and commitment/no commitment:

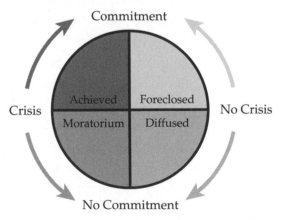

Figure 3.1 Adapted from James Marcia's Typology[7]

If a student is not exploring identity in a particular area (meaning she has experienced no "crisis"), she either moves toward *diffusion* (no commitment) or *foreclosure* (premature commitment). On the other hand, if a crisis has catapulted her into some identity exploration but she has not yet made an identity commitment, she is in *moratorium* (a state of indecision). Once a commitment is made, she has reached identity *achievement*—at least in that particular area of exploration, and at least for now. (Commitments can change over time, launching the individual back into the moratorium stage.)

In your youth group you will most likely have students who are at each of these different stages. The 14-year-old girl who wanders in and out of your youth ministry as predictably as she wanders from relationship to relationship with guys is *diffused*. She's fine with being known as a youth group member, but she mostly wants to be known as someone's girlfriend. She's not looking to figure out who she really is—yet. If you think back to the two college freshmen from the start of the chapter, this is Katie—the young woman who put her Christian commitment "on the shelf" and spent most of her freshman year partying.

Foreclosed students have chosen to follow someone else's lead on who they are—usually the lead of their parents. They've adopted their parents' beliefs, practices, and suggestions without looking at the options available to them. In youth group, foreclosed students often present like they "have it all together" with God. She's like Tiffany at the beginning of chapter 1—the ninth grader who always showed up early at youth group to help. These youth are often placed in leadership positions in our groups. The problem is that their faith is founded in a relationship with a role model (usually a parent or youth pastor)—not God. So when tough questions or circumstances hit (such as Tiffany's unexpected pregnancy), these students haven't developed the personal relationship with God that would enable them to cling to him and continue to grow in the midst of the difficult events or challenges.

When you see a kid in your youth group who's listening to a different type of music every week, or wearing army fatigues one week and an artsy outfit the next, he's most likely in the midst of *moratorium.* Adolescents in this phase are *exploring* their options, moving toward commitment to a particular identity.

Achievement occurs when youth have processed their options and have decided on a genuine identity: one that is self-chosen and thought through. It's not a finished identity, but some firm commitments have been made. Perhaps you know some college students who have worked through this search and reclaimed their own genuine Christian identity—created in God's image, transformed by Christ's image. This might be the kid who quickly became overwhelmed by the pervasive party scene at college, forcing her to work out how she—not her parents—felt about drinking. This is Julia, the second of the two college freshmen at the beginning of this chapter.

Be warned, however, that even if a student has reached a certain degree of identity achievement, you might still see the other three of Marcia's stages of identity formation at work as well. This is one of the more confusing aspects of working with kids: Sometimes a student will astound you with adult-like maturity in one area, while simultaneously surprising you with another attitude or behavior that demonstrates shocking immaturity.

In these moments, you'll likely have two emotional responses: You'll get frustrated with the student, and you'll conclude that somehow it's your fault that the student keeps slipping. Rest assured, in today's complex and precarious world, all four of Marcia's categories happily play together in the developmental sandbox of most adolescents. As youth workers, it's our job to know that all of this conflicting, inconsistent, and confusing behavior is actually a student's way of discovering who he is and making the commitments toward who he wants to be.

Sadly, students often shove their faith into an "identity lockbox."

Sociologist Tim Clydesdale interviewed 125 students as they transitioned from high school to college.[8] He discovered that most college freshmen are overwhelmed by what he called "daily life management," meaning the juggling and maintenance of school and social networks (friends, authority figures, romantic partners). Rather than dive into figuring out who they are (the identity task), students store away important parts of who they are (often including, but not limited to, their religious and spiritual identities) in an "identity lockbox" when they enter college. For those who embrace the lockbox approach, college life is simply a series of disconnected events—without connection to one's true self and without regard to previous commitments, including faith.

Similarly, several of the students I (Cheryl) interviewed for our study acknowledged that they had put their faith on hold when they entered college so they could "enjoy the college life." Translated, that means *party*. When I asked them about shelving their faith, a couple of them acknowledged the inconsistency of it all. "I know it doesn't make sense. If I kick God to the curb for four years just so I can have fun, then why would I pick him up again? Obviously I don't think he's worthwhile, or I wouldn't dog him in the first place. I mean, we *are* talking about God, right?" Right.

Remember Katie and Julia from the beginning of this chapter? Katie placed her relationship with God in an identity lockbox. She simply thought there were more important things for her to think about. Putting her faith in her lockbox allowed her to drink and smoke pot without feeling guilty. Katie made a conscious decision to sideline her faith so she could "enjoy" college life.

Julia, on the other hand, unpacked her faith along with all of her worldly possessions when she arrived at college. One of the most difficult decisions for her regarded whether she would drink alcohol. Coming from a teetotaling family, she had decided before entering college that she would not drink at all. During fall semester she became very aware of the primacy of alcohol on her campus—at all the parties. After a lot of discussion with her roommate, they decided together that in order to continue developing friendships with others in their dorm, they would attend the parties and have one drink each. You may or may not agree with the wisdom of her decision, but Julia was engaging her faith identity as part of her decision-making process.

There are many pitfalls to a lockbox approach to faith during college, but we need only mention three here. First, when students put their faith on hold while in college, they are easily pushed by the shifting winds of their college culture. The party scene, including drinking alcohol, smoking pot, and engaging in casual sexual encounters, is a major force on college campuses—more than you might think (even Christian colleges). Second, when students set aside their faith for a time, it affects the quality of their integrated thinking. Can youth really make true-to-self decisions about their worldviews, romantic partners, career directions, or graduate school if they've placed their faith on hold? Finally, there's the issue of what happens when students finally bust open those lockboxes and take a serious look at who they are, either some time later in college or perhaps after they've completed the college experience. Many will face deep regret about the decisions they've made.

Each student's identity is ultimately rooted in God's love and call.

In the midst of the challenges of the identity process, your students will inevitably battle with two seemingly competing forces: the need to be seen and valued as unique and different, while at the same time longing to be wanted and to belong. God's view of our core identity satisfies these two driving identity needs.

Well-known Roman Catholic priest and author Henri Nouwen proposed that the answer to the single most important question affecting all of humanity, "Who am I?", is the message of Jesus and the Bible.[9] Each of your students has been created, redeemed, and called to live as God's precious and beloved child. Nouwen suggested that true identity is discovered as we hear the voice of God calling us "the beloved." Nouwen wrote that the phrase "You are my beloved" reveals "the most intimate truth about all human beings."[10]

A 16-year-old guy in your youth ministry may be good at many things, and he may bring you and others great joy as his personality develops. A 14-year-old girl may show amazing promise as you watch her grow into a young woman with a lot to offer the world. But every kid we work with is more than the sum of his or her abilities, gifts, and personality traits. At the very core, each of them is the *beloved child of God.*

The practical work of centering yourself and your students in being God's beloved is a lifelong process. Although the majority of the work of sorting out who you are is accomplished through adolescence and emerging adulthood, you and your students will continue to work out your sense of God's love throughout your entire lives.[11]

Sticky Faith Made Practical

Who am I? What do I want to do with my life? Where do I belong?

Students engage these and other key questions of the identity formation process in different ways and on different timetables. Much of the spiritual identity process is mysterious and particularized, as is so characteristic of our loving God and Creator. But given how influential kids' relationships are, you are well positioned to make a difference in their identity formation. What can you as a youth worker do to help students live through these years of transition with a sense of being God's beloved, rather than delaying the development process or placing faith in a lockbox?

Develop rituals and rites of passage.

Churches are in a unique position to support people through meaningful life transitions. This means your youth ministry has the potential to be a unique crucible for students' faith identity exploration.[12] How does this work?

Pastor and theologian Will Willimon reminds us, "Ritual—patterned, purposeful, predictable behavior—is a component of all Christian worship . . . Ritual does things for us that cannot be done any other way."[13] What ritual mostly does is *teach* us—and that's whether our rituals involve brushing our teeth after every meal, raising our hands during worship, or kneeling on little benches under a pew. Rituals tell us who we are, and because churches involve so many rituals in worship and rites of passage, they provide an environment unlike any other, where our stories are caught up into the stories of others and the Story of God.

Rites of passage and other faith rituals need not be ancient to be effective in transmitting identity and a sense of God's love, though we can leverage wisdom from historic practices. The truth is that improvisation is part of every ritual. Even rituals that endure across time are reinvented to some extent each time they are used.[14]

Perhaps your denominational tradition practices a vibrant confirmation process, or one that can be revitalized with new purpose. Or maybe you're part of a church absent of any significant rites of passage. Here are some opportunities that could encourage students in their identity development process:

Rites for entering and leaving adolescence

The words *middle school* and *junior high* don't really communicate the significance of this life change, and kids need more than the trial-by-fire of walking down the halls of their new school to serve as an initiation into this journey. Similarly, graduation from high school may not mark the end of adolescence, but rituals that confer "adult status"—or at least acknowledge emerging adulthood—spur the process of taking on an adult identity within the community. Retreats, parent-child experiences, or special worship rituals can communicate that a child is entering into adolescence, and that an adolescent is entering adulthood. The church family must then recognize that young person's new status. Some churches have found the following rituals effective for celebrating the beginning and end of adolescence:

- Wilderness trips of varying degrees (from an overnight campout to much longer backpacking adventures) can be useful rituals to enact physically the symbolic journeying taking place in kids' lives. For instance, a group of 12-year-old boys or girls on a week-long canoeing trip are led through the course of the week to see themselves leaving the land of childhood and entering new territory as teenagers.

- Other rites of passage can happen within the congregation. In some African-American churches, parents give their kids bread to eat and recite a liturgy that confers the status of adulthood to them, proclaiming that they are now adults who must feed themselves both physically and spiritually, though they will not have to do so alone.[15]

- Gender-specific rites of passage are marvelous tools to help confer the identity of son or daughter of God. For instance, you might provide girls with mirrors and some fingernail polish and have them paint the words "God's image" on their mirror as a daily reminder of the only true source of one's image and identity. Or have a group of men mentor boys in specific ways over the course of a year (spiritually, relationally, and building practical skills) and then celebrate together with a meal and blessing.

See chapter 8 on preparing for more specific ritual ideas for seniors who are graduating from your group.

Rituals to acknowledge milestones

Certain *cultural milestones*, such as getting a driver's license, turning 16, or graduating from high school, are times for both celebration and demarcation. What practice could you initiate that would say, "We celebrate that you have come to this point of transition, and we will continue to walk with you as you face the challenges of your journey"? For example, when a kid in your youth ministry gets their learner's permit or driver's license, don't just kid about it and say, "Everybody better watch out on the roads!" Instead, invite the whole community to pray for that young person, noting the significance of this cultural milestone. Pray for growing discernment as she makes driving choices that can carry heavy consequences, for safety as she navigates dangerous moments on the road, and for grace as she handles the new freedom and responsibility that driving brings.

Spiritual milestones, though not as connected with the life cycle, can be coupled with rites of passage. Look carefully at how your church celebrates baptisms and confessions of faith in Christ. Without exploiting kids' spiritual journeys or putting them on display, give them meaningful opportunities to publicly proclaim their faith. Celebrate that they are now part of the family of God broadly and the family of your church specifically, maybe by following every baptism with a big church family meal or a big party at a local park.

Ritual meals

Across nearly all cultures, eating and drinking together serves as a rite of incorporation and of union. It is a sacred act. Jesus seemed eager to share a meal with just about anyone—so much so that he was considered by some to be a glutton and a heavy drinker! (Luke 7:34) Do the people of your church welcome kids to their tables? Does the community find reasons to celebrate kids with grand banquets or even small ceremonies of table fellowship?

Christians view communion as the ritual meal of greatest significance. Yet in many churches, youth are unintentionally excluded from participation in this ritual because of programming decisions. If your church's schedule prevents kids from participating in the Lord's Supper with other believers, consider shifting the timing of your worship or youth ministry program to make their participation possible. Even better, involve them in serving the elements, or periodically include a blessing for teenagers during communion.

Identify your kids' passions and gifts.

Youth workers complain about kids being too busy, with schedules crammed with activities 24/7. Rather than add to the busyness by offering a slew of programs, youth ministries can instead provide strategic activities to help youth explore their interests, abilities, and gifts.

The Search Institute, having studied more than 3 million kids over the past 30 years, calls these passionate interests "sparks." Sparks give life meaning, focus, energy, and joy. Search has found that sparks are particularly powerful in kids' lives when: (1) kids know their particular sparks, (2) the sparks are important to them, and (3) they take initiative to develop those sparks. Unfortunately, only about half of teens know and are developing their sparks.[16]

When you see a student's eyes light up during an experience, take note. Do you have a volunteer or is there an adult in the church who has that same interest or ability? Figure out a way to connect the two of them in the context of their shared interest. For instance, young filmmakers might connect with the church media team to contribute their creativity and tech savvy. Or a kid who loves to build things could team up with a group of retired construction workers to build ramps at the homes of people with disabilities.

Help kids learn to reflect on their experiences.

Each time I (Cheryl) interviewed students over four college years, they thanked me for challenging them to reflect on their college experience. They told me that no one else had ever asked what was happening to them as they navigated college. Taking time to reflect is something we need to be intentional about both before and after graduation.

When I directed a leadership development program for high school students several years ago, I gave a journal to each student. After every experience and every Bible study, the staff scheduled time for students to reflect and record their thoughts. Even at the end of a long trip or all-day activity, we always eked out a few extra minutes, just so students could *process* what they'd heard, seen, or experienced. No lockbox was available—just engagement.

Our world is very fast-paced and full of data. It's only when we schedule "time-outs" for reflection that kids can truly process. And it's only in reflection that they'll do the work required for identity formation.

Pay attention to trigger events that promote identity growth.

In other research on faith development among college students, significant struggles have often been revealed as major catalysts for faith growth.[17] We can be looking out for particular "trigger" events that could create the kinds of internal crises that lead to identity growth, such as:

1. Exposure to diverse ways of thinking. When other students, classes, or other sources stir up different ways of thinking or believing, these moments can spur critical growth.
2. Multicultural exposure through mission trips, living in another culture, befriending someone from another culture, or even reading about people from other cultures.
3. Relationship, health, or emotional challenges like significant illness, conflict with parents, or other negative experiences.

In her classic study on crisis and faith, Margaret Hall discovered that those who showed the most spiritual depth after experiencing crises were those who had consciously reoriented their faith in order to overcome the crisis. In other words, they were attentive to the ways their faith must change so they could climb out of the pit of despair.[18] Students in the throes of adolescence may need our help to both recognize and walk through the faith transformation that can come about in response to such trigger events.

Seek variety in adult leaders.

If you are like most youth leaders, you probably find it's easier to recruit volunteers who are just like you. They think like you, they value the same things you do, and sometimes they even dress like you. You don't have to explain yourself to them very often because they're so much like you—they just get it.

But that's not what's best for kids. We need to attract a diverse team of youth workers—old and young, with a range of interests and strengths. Students will then have the opportunity to hear stories of others' lives, opening the door for them to think further about the options available in their own lives. Being in relationship with a variety of adults enables youth to see how God works uniquely in each life. It prevents your kids from assuming that being a Christian requires that they look, act, and think just like you; instead, it frees them up to investigate who they can be as Christians.

Steve is a youth leader whom I would describe as very organized, passionate, and relational. Music is *not* his gift. But he successfully recruited another team member (Nico) who not only plays guitar, but also is a skilled worship leader. Thanks to Nico, the youth ministry has expanded to include and encourage musical students who want to hone their skills and learn how to lead people in worship—something Steve could not do. And let's not ignore the relational impact Nico is having simply by being himself and connecting to students more like him.

> My relationship with God since leaving high school has been a roller coaster. At first, it may sound like a negative thing, but it isn't necessarily. We all need those little dips in order to bring ourselves to a higher understanding of God's glory and power.
>
> —Jamari

> For more on recruiting youth leaders, see chapter 7, "Sticky Youth Groups."

Support stability in your adult leadership team: Go for 4+1

Remember Julia from the beginning of this chapter? One reason she was able to sustain her faith through college was the strong foundation of long-term relationships she had with adults in her church. Every week since they were in junior high school, Julia and her friend Mary had been meeting with Lora, their small group leader. Even after their college graduations, Lora is involved in their lives via email, phone calls, and texts. Therefore, Julia had not only the benefit of a good friend in multiple contexts, but also the extraordinarily rare joy of having an invested adult walk with her through life since she was 12.

Our research suggests we need to consider a new model for Sticky Youth Ministry: **4+1.** For high school ministries, this formula means the four years between ninth and twelfth grade plus *one additional year.* Rather than shifting all of our attention away from seniors after they complete high school, it makes more sense to continue ministering to them throughout their first year of college or work. According to our research, an additional year of contact with an adult from the high school ministry, even though the contact is almost certain to be less intensive and less regular, could provide critical support during one of the most difficult transitions they will face. In fact, that contact continues to make a difference two years later. What if we began recruiting volunteers by sharing this 4+1 strategy as part of the vision for their ongoing influence in kids' lives?

Those of us who work with students throughout their high school years already invest a great deal of time and effort to help students accept that they are God's beloved. Wouldn't it make sense to stick with students a bit longer to gain a more long-term kingdom return on that investment? I bet Katie and Julia—as well as the kids in your ministry—would sure appreciate it.

sticky discussion questions

1. How does your youth ministry currently help students process the questions "Who am I?" and "Who am I as a part of us?"

2. In what ways have you seen graduates from your youth ministry put their faith in an identity lockbox—or not?

3. Do you agree with the idea that the first year of college is a lot like redoing middle school? Why or why not? How are the two life stages similar? How are they different?

4. What "sparks" are you seeing in your students? To whom could you connect them in order to develop those sparks further?

5. Take a look at your volunteer youth leaders. Do they look, think, and live just like you do? How could you recruit people who are *different* from you to reach and embrace students who are also different from you?

6. What would 4 + 1 look like in your setting? How could you make that fifth year more feasible and appealing for your youth leaders?

4

sticky churches

My church made me feel like a valued part of the congregation, like an adult.
—Keely

The students seemed to be very separated from the rest of the congregation. Maybe fixing that gap would help unite the church.
—Delonte

I've been so thankful for the people who have surrounded my life and who have mentored me and encouraged me because I've gotten to see examples of what a Christian woman is and what a godly woman and a godly man are.
—Tara

I (Kara) am the oldest of 15 cousins on my dad's side of the family. For family holidays during my youth, 30 of my relatives would gather at Grandma and Grandpa Eckmann's house for family holidays. That's far too many people to fit around one table.

So we set up two tables: the adults' table and the kids' table.

We Eckmanns are far from the only family to arrive at this clever and practical "two table" solution. I'm sure many of you are nodding as you think about the two tables at your own family gatherings.

At Grandma and Grandpa Eckmann's, the adults ate in the dining room. We kids ate in the TV room.

The adults sat at the fancy dining room table. We sat around card tables.

They ate off nice china. We ate off paper plates or, if we were lucky, plastic ones.

They were all given napkins—cloth napkins at that. We used our shirtsleeves.

They had pleasant conversations. Somehow our talks usually degenerated into throwing dinner rolls at one another and having a Jell–O snorting contest.

In theory, we were all at the same meal. In reality, the adults and the kids had very different experiences.

That sounds a lot like how many of us experience church today. The adults' table is in the bigger, nicer room; the kids' table is down the hall.

Most churches have adult pastors . . . and youth pastors.

Adult worship services . . . and youth worship services.

Adult mission trips . . . and youth mission trips.

Do 16-year-olds need time to be together and on their own? You bet. As one youth worker told me, "The average 16-year-old guy doesn't want to talk about masturbation with Grandma in the room." Neither does Grandma. So that's a win-win.

But one of my life mantras says, "Balance is something we swing through on our way to the other extreme." And I'm afraid that's what's happened here. In our effort to offer relevant and developmentally appropriate teaching and fellowship for teenagers, we have segregated—and I use that verb intentionally but not lightly—youth from the rest of the church. As one student in our study lamented, "So, it was kind of . . . I don't like this word, but for lack of a better one, segregated, in the sense of the high school students have their thing and then the adults have their thing."

And that segregation is causing students to shelve their faith.

Sticky Findings

Greatness Jesus-Style = Adults + Children

I remember the first Bible I received as a child. On the cover was a picture of a very Anglo-Saxon looking Jesus surrounded by smiling children of all different skin colors. Jesus had this dewy glow, and I think there were fluffy sheep nibbling on tufts of grass in the background. Too cute.

In reality, Jesus' vision for intergenerational relationships was anything but cute. It was—and is—both radical and revolutionary.

In Luke 9:28-36, Jesus takes Peter, James, and John to a mountain to pray. Jesus' selection of only those three disciples almost certainly fueled feelings of jealousy and insecurity among the nine left behind. I can almost hear the other disciples grumbling under their breath, "What makes Peter so dang special?"

Soon after, an argument breaks out among all 12 of Jesus' disciples about who is the greatest. It seems Jesus didn't actually hear their argument for Luke writes that "knowing their thoughts, [Jesus] took a little child and had him stand beside him" (9:47). Jesus continues, "Whoever welcomes this little child in my name welcomes me; and whoever welcomes me welcomes the one who sent me. For it is the one who is least among you all who is the greatest" (9:48).

Thus Jesus placed two figures before the disciples: himself, whom they greatly respected, and a child, who held little intrinsic value in

> My family had moved away when I turned about 16, so the church adults became like my family; and I would go over to their houses and just really engage in a lot of good conversations. I got a lot of my mentorship from the personal interaction with a lot of the adults from my church. And just spending time at their houses, watching them do family devotions, watching them even interact and do chores, I learned a lot about a stable family life . . . It's where I spend most of my time.
>
> —Marc

their culture. The good news for the disciples was that greatness could be pursued and possessed. The bad news for the disciples is that greatness comes from doing something counterintuitive: welcoming a child.

The Greek word Jesus used in this familiar statement about intergenerational relationships made his teaching all the more difficult for the disciples to swallow. The Greek verb Jesus uses that gets translated as "welcome" is *dechomai* (pronounced "DECK-oh-my"), which often meant showing hospitality to guests. Thus, it carried a certain connotation of servanthood. In the first century, taking care of both guests and children was a task generally fulfilled by those whom the culture viewed as different from, and even inferior to, the male disciples—meaning women and slaves.[1]

Jesus asked the disciples who had just been arguing about their individual greatness to show utmost humility by embracing the kids in their midst. According to Jesus, greatness—and dare we say "great" ministry and "great" churches—emerges as adults welcome children.

The first-century vision for "church" was all about people, not about a building.

Now fast-forward a few years from Jesus to the ministry of the apostle Paul. When Paul describes "church" in his letters, he uses the Greek word *ekklesia*, which means literally "those who are called out." According to Paul, the church is *people* who have been set apart.

Think for a moment how far we've drifted from that early definition of *church*. Today when we talk about "church," most of the time we're talking about a building. We'll say, "I'm going to church on Sunday." In our minds, church is a destination, a place.

For Paul, that would be heresy.

For Paul, the church is a living, active group of people—people of all ages—who are called by God to live according to kingdom values and priorities. You and I can't understand what it means to be part of a Sticky Church that develops long-term faith in kids unless we understand that church is not about buildings, or programs, or activities, or budgets—it's about people.

Involvement in all-church worship during high school is more consistently linked with mature faith in both high school and college than any other form of church participation.

As we planned our College Transition Project, our FYI research team had hoped to find *one thing* youth workers could *do* that would be the "silver bullet" of Sticky Faith. We were searching for that *one element* of youth ministry programming (i.e., small groups, mentoring, justice work) that was significantly related to higher faith maturity—standing head and shoulders above the rest.

We haven't found that silver bullet. While small groups, mentoring, justice work, and a host of other youth ministry programs are important, the reality is that the challenges of kids, ministry programs, and spiritual development are far too complicated to be met with a single solution. There's no cure-all.

The closest our research has come to that definitive silver bullet is this sticky finding: High school and college students who experience more intergenerational worship tend to have higher faith maturity. We found this to be true in our studies of both high school seniors AND college freshmen.

The more teenagers serve and build relationships with younger children, the more likely it is that their faith will stick.

Granted, some of your teenagers may opt to serve in children's ministry because they want to avoid going to "big church." Others may volunteer in children's ministry because their school requires service hours.

Yet even amid these mixed motives, the students we surveyed who had served in middle school or children's ministry while they were in high school seemed to have stickier faith in college. Part of

Some Theological Principles Behind Intergenerational Youth Ministry

by David Fraze[2]

"Hear, O Israel: The LORD our God, the LORD is one . . ."
—Deuteronomy 6:4

Most of us have probably read, sang, contemplated, and perhaps even memorized this passage of Scripture. A deeper examination of Deuteronomy 6:4-9 reveals several important principles of intergenerational philosophy for youth ministry.

- *Parents and the surrounding community of adults are expected to exemplify what it means to be fully devoted followers of God.* The expectation of total devotion is indicated in several portions of the Deuteronomy 6 passage. To declare "The LORD our God, the LORD is one . . ." is no small matter. Research shows, whether for good or bad, children follow the spiritual lead set by their parents and surrounding adult community.
- *Adults, starting with parents, are commanded to be active participants in their children's spiritual formation.* The phrase "Impress them on your children" indicates parents' responsibility and agreement to teach their children about the Lord. The action verbs that follow the command to "impress" indicate constant process and interaction.

Jesus' experience and teachings mirror and often intensify the principles of intergenerational ministry already highlighted from Deuteronomy 6:4-9.

- The obedience of the cross is evidence enough that *Jesus lived life as a fully devoted follower of God.* Jesus requires the same full, cross-bearing devotion from those who make the commitment to follow him (Luke 14:26-27).
- *Jesus spoke of adults as active participants in a child's spiritual formation.* Jesus strongly opposed the disciples who were attempting to keep children away from him (Mark 10:13-14).
- *Jesus welcomed children into his crowded schedule* and urged others to do the same in his name (Matthew 18:5).

that is probably due to the type of student likely to volunteer to serve younger children. Nonetheless, older kids' involvement in children's ministry seems to be more than just baby-sitting; it is faith-building.[3]

High school seniors don't feel supported by adults in their congregations.

As a research team, we weren't all that surprised that of five major sources of support (adults in the congregation, parents, youth workers, friends in youth group, and friends outside of youth group), high school seniors ranked the adults in the congregation last.

What *did* surprise us was *how far behind* the other four groups the congregational adults were. One youth group graduate reported that his church "would like to talk about having students involved, but they never really did." Another reflected that church members "wanted nothing to do with us . . . I think they see us as kind of scary in that we're the people on the news, you know, who are dealing drugs and . . . um . . . getting pregnant and all those sort of things . . . keeping us separate and treating us like we were a hazard."

By far, the number one way churches made the teens in our survey feel welcomed and valued was when adults in the congregation showed an interest in them.

More than any program or event, what made kids more likely to feel like a significant part of their local church was when adults made the effort to get to know them. One student beamed, "We were welcomed not just in youth group, we were welcomed into other parts of the ministry of the church, whether it be in the worship or the praise team on Sunday mornings, or whether it be teaching Sunday school to kids or helping with cleaning and serving. . . . All these other types of things really just brought the youth in and made them feel like they had a place and even feel like they were valued as individuals."

One student who grew up in a small, multigenerational church spoke of the special relationship he'd developed with the 80-year-old mayor of his town. Each time Daniel returned home from college, she met with him for coffee or lunch, just so they could talk. Daniel commented, "I can talk about anything with her . . . She goes out of her way to find me." When Daniel's mother was diagnosed with breast cancer, the mayor became like a godmother to him. Interestingly, Daniel's pseudo-godmother was the one who invited him to teach children's Sunday school, which he now does every time he is home. Daniel is fully "stuck" to the life of his small, intergenerational church.

Contact from adults in the church makes a difference.

Contrary to public opinion, graduates don't want to be "out of sight, out of mind." Contact from at least one adult from the congregation *outside of the youth ministry* during the first semester of college is linked with Sticky Faith. Hearing from an adult from their home church—whether it be via text, email, phone, or something you've perhaps heard of called "the U.S. Postal Service"—seems to help students take their faith to college with them. In fact, that ongoing contact still makes a difference three years later.

One of the top three difficulties students face as they journey to college is finding a church.

Once they became college freshmen, we asked the seniors in our study to share their top difficulties after graduation. Here's what they told us:

- Number 1 was friendship.
- Number 2 was aloneness.
- Number 3 was finding a church.

It's no wonder students have a hard time finding a church after high school. Those who have been sitting at the youth ministry "kids' table" may know youth group, but often they don't know the church at all.

Sticky Faith Made Practical

Our good friend and colleague, Dr. Chap Clark, says a lot of brilliant things. But we think perhaps his most brilliant insight in the last few years is that we need to "reverse the youth ministry ratio."

What does he mean?

Chap is talking about the ratio of adults-to-kids involved in a church youth program. Churches often talk about seeking a 1:5 ratio of adults to kids (meaning one adult for every five kids) for its small groups. For bigger youth events (such as a winter youth retreat), a youth ministry might feel comfortable with a 1:7 ratio of adults to kids.

What if we reversed that? What if instead of talking about one adult for every five (or seven) kids involved, we said we want a 5:1 adult-to-kid ratio in our youth ministries? Before you panic and say that's completely unrealistic, let me clarify: I'm not talking about five adult small group leaders for every student. I'm talking about five adults who are willing to commit to invest in one teenager in little, medium, and big ways. According to one study, teens who had five or more adults from the church invested in them during the ages of 15 to 18 were less likely to leave the church after high school.[4] As we at FYI connect with churches across the country, we have seen churches embrace 5:1 in ways that transform their church cultures and ministry programs.

Changing Your Church Culture

Last month I (Kara) went away for an overnighter with my account-ability group. Blanca, Amy, and Robyn are among my dearest friends, and we're never short on conversation topics. We went out for lunch . . . and talked. We went for a walk along the beach . . . and talked. We went shopping . . . and talked. We stopped at a nice res-taurant for dinner . . . and talked. We woke up the next morning . . . and talked. It was a glorious weekend.

But for me, there was one disappointment that marred what was otherwise a relaxing and charming weekend. We decided to visit a church in the beach town in which we were staying. There was much I liked about the church. The worship music was engaging. The pastoral team had a vision for planting churches and justice work in the community. They served Starbucks tea and coffee.

The researcher in me has realized that you can tell a lot about a church by its bulletin. And when I decided to peruse the bulletin, there in the midst of announcements regarding various exciting opportunities for service and outreach, I found a note labeled "Limiting Distractions." Here's what it said:

> We kindly ask each person's help in limiting distractions during the church service. It is our desire to provide distraction-free ministry at all services. Therefore, while in the sanctuary, please turn off your cell phones. We request that children under the age of 12 attend their age-appropriate classes, for their benefit and that of the entire body.

I'm guessing the church's intention was to provide a focused worship experience; and on one level, there's nothing wrong with that. But what did that cost the congregation? There's no way that church can experience a new 5:1 ratio if the church culture views kids under 12 as distractions who should be silenced and put away like cell phones.

Maybe your church isn't that blatant in segregating its youth. My church, Lake Avenue Church, is working toward more intergenera-

I had grown up in the church and felt pretty welcome there, and I even got to play drums on the worship team once when the regular drummer wasn't there, even though I wasn't very good. I just knew that even as a teenager, I could connect with everyone at the church from differing ages. The church was one big family. There were potlucks in which everyone participated. Everyone who attended the church was at every event, helping out with each other and building relationships.

—Dennis

tional worship and relationships. But a few years ago, my daughter (who was six at the time) showed me how far we still have to go.

It was Good Friday, and our family arrived a few minutes early for the evening service. As we were waiting for the service to start, Krista pointed at the front of the worship center and asked, "Mommy, what are those yellow tubes? There are so many of them."

I smiled and answered, "Krista, those are the pipes for the organ."

"Mommy, what's an organ?"

My amusement at my daughter's first question quickly changed to dismay. No one, including me, had ever explained to her all of the dynamics and elements of our worship service. How could she feel a part of the broader community if she felt like a confused outsider?

So I made it my mission at that Good Friday service to explain everything. I whispered in her ear, "Hear that music? That's coming from the organ."

"See that woman? She's making announcements . . ."

"Can you read those words on the screen? They're reminding us what Jesus did by dying for us on the cross."

Here I am, a champion for intergenerational ministry, and my own daughter didn't understand what was happening in intergenerational worship. It was a good reminder that we grown-ups take a lot for granted.

Sticky Church culture often flows from the top.

Why is it so important to try to get the support of pastoral leadership? After all, if you're like me, you're a major believer in the priesthood of all believers. As Martin Luther and the Reformers helped us understand five centuries ago, the role of "minister" is not limited to those who are vocational or bivocational ministers. God invites all of God's followers to use their gifts in kingdom work.

Having said that, the reality is that church culture generally flows from the top. If your senior pastor values and participates in authentic relationships, your church is more likely to experience that type of community. If your senior pastor has a heart for those who are poor, your church is more likely to be involved in justice work.

X Marks the Spot

One idea FYI suggests for churches that want to change their culture is to develop an "intergenerational map" of their church campus. Here's how you can make an intergenerational map for your ministry:[5]

1. Gather a group of parents, kids, youth ministry volunteers, and church leaders who are interested in changing the church culture.
2. Explain to them the vision behind a new 5:1 ratio.
3. Using a big sheet of poster paper, draw a picture of the path that the typical teenager takes from the moment she arrives in the parking lot at a typical church gathering (e.g., Sunday morning) until the time that gathering ends and she drives out of that same parking spot. Make sure to include teenage hotspots like the bathrooms, available food (especially free food), and any other places where kids tend to congregate.
4. Ask the group to mark with an X all the points in this path where your students interact with adults.
5. Remind them of the 5:1 vision and invite them to identify additional points along the path that could be catalysts for greater adult-kid interaction. Draw a star on the map at each of these locations.
6. Identify which of the stars on the map are most doable, as well as which stars are most likely to have the greatest effect on teenagers.
7. Determine which stars to focus on and what action steps you need to take to turn those sites into hubs that get you closer to 5:1.
8. If you are meeting at or near the site depicted in your map, close your training with a prayer walk. Follow the footsteps of a typical student in your ministry and pray for 5:1 adult-student interaction along the way. If you are not meeting on location, close in prayer by gathering around the map you have drawn and focusing on locations marked by an X or a star.
9. Keep the map and review it later as a team. If you have the opportunity, present the map to other pastors and leadership groups at your church as a powerful visual of both the current state of adult-kid interaction, as well as the potential for Sticky Relationships.

The same is true for intergenerational ministry.

I am thrilled that the senior pastor at our church, Dr. Greg Way-bright, is a champion of diversity of all sorts—race, gender, socio-economic status, and . . . you guessed it . . . age, too. And I love that his interest in diversity doesn't flow from either a sense of guilt or a desire to be "politically correct." He's realized that from Genesis to Revelation, God has invited us to be in relationships that transcend typical cultural barriers.

When Greg first joined our church, he would regularly email our youth pastors after our weekend services, asking something like, "I met a girl from Arcadia High School at church this weekend. She plays the violin. I don't remember her name but I'd like to shoot her an email. Can you please get me her name and email address?" I'm proud to be part of a church community led by a senior pastor who is so committed to intergenerational relationships.

> So like they allowed youth to be part of the worship team in church service. The new senior pastor would come to youth group and talk with us and visit small groups and invite us to the church service personally, so we all started going to the church service, too.
>
> —Carolina

But what do you do if your senior pastor isn't on board the intergenerational train? We'll get back to this in more depth in chapter 9, but in the meantime, perhaps you can give her a copy of this book and ask her to pay special attention to this chapter and its Sticky Findings. Or maybe you invite him to an event that's designed to be intergenerational and debrief the experience afterward, discussing how it felt to have 16- and 66-year-olds together. Time spent communicating your Sticky Faith vision with other leaders is *never* wasted.

Changing Your Ministry Programming

Nuancing What You Already Do

As you intentionally move your programs toward a new 5:1 ratio, the good news is that you don't have to start from scratch. Your youth ministry and your church are already hosting events that, with some careful planning, could easily become more intergenerational.

So get out your youth ministry calendar and identify which events have potential for more 5:1 interaction.

Maybe you invite an adult Sunday school class to join you for part or all of your next mission trip.

Or your youth baptism service at a neighborhood swimming pool becomes a children's and youth baptism service.

Or you invite students' parents to your summer kick-off.

Then take a look at the calendar of events for your broader church. Perhaps you encourage your guys' small groups to attend the men's annual steak fry. (What is a steak fry? Do men literally fry steaks at these events? I've never been to one.).

Or you ask your women's ministries if their upcoming Saturday Tea can be geared for teenage and younger girls too.

Or you see if your senior adult ministry would be open to pairing up with teenagers for the next food pantry program.

The bottom line is that if you plan ahead, you can capitalize on momentum from existing events instead of starting them all from scratch. Whenever possible, explain your 5:1 vision to the adults at these events so they can get on board and help students feel welcome.

5:1 Teaching

It's critical to build on what the church is already doing. But if you're serious about sticky intergenerational relationships, you'll probably need to launch a few new catalysts for 5:1. One good opportunity for new 5:1 dialogue is your Sunday teaching. Odds are good that you've got adults and kids sitting in Sunday school rooms separated only by a few walls. (And, as a youth worker, you hope those walls have really good sound insulation.) What if you removed those walls—metaphorically, or maybe even literally—by inviting kids and adults to periodically experience God's Word together?

Last fall my church held a six-week Sunday school class on "Christ and Culture" that combined specially invited high school upperclassmen with senior adults. Some of the most meaningful 5:1 moments in the class were when the teenagers showed how they were trying to shape culture. One kid brought his guitar and played a song he'd written. Another youth wants to be a fashion designer and brought in sketches of her clothes. The kids had the chance to share their talents and visions, and then the senior adults ooh'ed and aah'ed over the kids' gifts and asked them how their faith shapes their work.

5:1 Worship

Another church I heard about is taking larger leaps toward sticky intergenerational relationships through their worship. Like many youth ministries, the youth program at this congregation had always met twice a week—once on Sundays and once on Wednesdays. The youth pastor, along with some kids, parents, and other church leaders, started asking, "Why do we meet twice a week? What's the purpose of each meeting?"

They realized they were more or less offering the same sort of worship, teaching, and fellowship twice every week. They also realized that very few of their students were involved in the larger church.

> They tried once a year doing a student-led service where we'd kind of organize what was going to be said and the music and everything. And some of the volunteers that were involved with helping us . . . showed us their encouragement in how we grew, not just as Christians, but how we grew as a church, and how we could make the church grow. But we also had some that kind of pushed us away, too. Like some of them didn't think we were mature enough to take on that kind of responsibility.
>
> —Cory

So they canceled Sunday youth group. No more Sunday meetings. Instead, kids are now fully integrated into the larger church on Sundays. Kids are greeters; they serve alongside adults in the worship music team; they offer testimonies; they even give chunks of the sermon from time to time. Commenting on the power of this 5:1 shift, the youth pastor noted: "We knew that this would change our kids. What has surprised us is how much it has changed our church."

Another church I dialogued with recently wants adults and kids to experience the same worship service every week, but they also want to make sure the teenagers feel connected to their peers. So every Sunday after the intergenerational worship service ends, the high school students meet for 30 to 45 minutes to talk about how to live out the sermon during that next week at school. That way students know they'll have a focused, lively conversation with their friends every week.

In an effort to bring a sticky intergenerational flavor to morning worship, another church decided to make its youth choir the primary choir for the 11 a.m. Sunday service. They knew there was some risk that the service would shrink in size until the teenagers and their parents were the only ones attending. But the opposite ended up happening. That 11 a.m. service became one of the church's most popular services, as adults who'd invested in those kids over the years as Sunday school teachers and confirmation sponsors, as well as other adults who simply cared about kids, couldn't wait to have the teenagers lead them in worship music.

We're not saying that every church should cancel its Sunday youth group or disband the adult choir. But we are saying that every church should ask: How can we increase adult-kid interaction during worship?

The way one church answered that question provides a powerful and sticky image of how kids can and should be involved through worship. One Sunday, the regular music team comprised solely of adults stepped forward at the beginning of worship and began singing and playing their instruments. Just like normal.

Suddenly, a teenager came forward from the congregation and tapped the shoulder of the guitarist. The kid held out both hands, and the adult guitarist handed his guitar to the kid and promptly walked off the platform. The kid immediately started playing the guitar.

A few moments later, another kid came up and tapped the adult drummer on the shoulder. The same thing happened: The drummer stood up, handed his sticks to the kid, and walked off the platform. The kid took over and resumed drumming.

Within a few minutes, kids had stepped up and taken the places of the bass player, keyboardist, and lead singer. What started as an all-adult worship team had become an all-youth worship team. And church members of all ages were swept up in a new spirit of enthusiastic worship.

But it didn't end there. A few minutes into the senior pastor's sermon, a voice called out, "If you're serious about involving us, we have to go all the way." Then a teenager appeared on the platform, walked up to the senior pastor, and tapped him on the shoulder. The pastor stopped preaching, gave the microphone to the kid, and walked off the platform. The kid finished the sermon.

There's something very powerful and beautiful about that sticky image. We're so used to kids being segregated "off in the youth room" that when we get glimpses of kids being involved in the full church, we know it's right. We know it leads to Sticky Faith.

As much as I love what this church did, if I could wave my Sticky Faith Wand (still looking at how to invent one of those, by the way), there's one thing I would change: I wish the adults and kids had actually led worship and preached together. After all, our research doesn't suggest that kids need to *replace* adults in leading worship. Our vision is that kids and adults lead worship *together*.

I had coffee this week with a pastor of family ministry who'd just finished planning his church's Senior Sunday—the one weekend each year when the kids lead worship and preach. Until recently, Senior Sunday had been viewed as a "week off" for the adult worship team and senior pastor. But this new family pastor has a vision for intergenerational worship. So for the first time ever, he told the worship department they couldn't have the "week off" but instead

About Music Styles in Worship

Of course, we can't talk about intergenerational worship without an honest dialogue about the age-old worship music debate. Odds are good that the music on your kids' iPods is a lot different than the music on your adults' iPods—or maybe more accurately, your adults' CD players (and maybe even cassette players).

One youth pastor in the state of Washington was under enormous pressure from his senior pastor to "get more kids" (love that language, by the way) to attend the church service. One of the primary reasons kids said they didn't want to attend worship was because they didn't like the church's organ music. The youth pastor tried to explain the concern to his senior pastor, but his explanation fell on deaf ears.

One day the youth pastor read a newspaper article about a shopping mall that was having a problem with teenagers loitering late at night after the mall was closed. The mall's solution was to install a sound system with speakers in the parking lot—and guess what they played at night to repel the teenagers? Organ music.

The very same music being used to repel students dominated the church's worship.

The youth pastor showed this article to the senior pastor, and the church started making some changes.

We admit we don't have a foolproof five- or ten-step plan to resolve the worship music debate. Some churches try to integrate different worship styles within one service (a little bit of electric guitar here, a little bit of organ there). Other churches try to come up with a worship style somewhere in the middle, which neither side totally loves but (hopefully) neither side hates either.

Finding the style of music that best suits your congregation is something each church must navigate based on its own context. But we can offer you this universal advice: You shouldn't try to steer that ship without getting a lot of input from both kids and adults, so everyone feels both heard and understood. Take time to build understanding and appreciation for difference so that even your discussions about varying preferences in worship style can contribute to your 5:1 momentum.

needed to be interspersed among the kids. While they grumbled at first, they soon caught the vision of Senior Sunday as a time to show the power of adults and kids praying, planning, and working *together* to lead the congregation in worship.

5:1 Mentoring

Many churches include mentoring in their 5:1 path. Through these empowering relationships, kids are able to spend intentional time with adults who are further along in their spiritual journeys. Our research has shown that the more adult mentors seek out a student and help the student apply faith to daily life, the better.[6]

In *The Slow Fade*, Reggie Joiner, Chuck Bomar, and Abbie Smith cast a new vision for mentoring. They write that mentors should ask, "What is God already doing here?" not, "What should God begin doing here?"[7] In this vision of 5:1 mentoring, adults who meet regularly with kids will often ask more questions and share more experiences than provide answers.

> For other tangible ideas on mentoring,
> visit www.stickyfaith.org.

Some youth leaders, realizing that the adults in their congregation are too busy to meet regularly with a teenager, have offered less intensive 5:1 connections. One Pasadena church in our Sticky Faith Learning Cohort is asking adults to commit a few hours per year to connect with a kid based on a mutual interest, such as gardening, cooking, or auto repair. Another Texas church in our Sticky Faith Learning Cohort identified members who might be too busy to commit to meeting with a teenager regularly for several years, but could probably meet weekly with a graduating senior for a few months. Because of that limited time commitment, they had great success in connecting youth group kids with innovative and godly congregation members of all ages.

Other churches are taking advantage of structures and programs that already combine kids with adults and infusing them with 5:1 mentoring vitality. At North Point Community Church in Georgia, teenagers serve at weekend worship services in a variety of ways, ranging from children's ministry volunteers to ushers and greeters. When possible, those teenagers are paired with an adult, making those adults a precious part of kids' growing 5:1 webs.

> I know this one woman—she's always praying for me and she's always telling me that she's praying for me . . . when I see her she's always asking me how I'm doing . . . that has meant so much for me, being two and half hours away at college, kinda out of sight and yet I'm not out of their minds.
>
> —Natalia

What do I do if I don't want the kids in my youth group to have the faith of the adults in my church?

This oh-so-sincere question from a committed local youth leader surprised me the first time I heard it in a conversation about 5:1 mentoring. Yet as I've shared this youth pastor's question with leaders across the country, I've come to realize that this is a common concern.

The good news is that your 5:1 mentoring doesn't have to be like a pinball game in which you launch kids toward a group of adults but then quickly lose all control over where (or who) they bounce against. Instead, think of your mentoring more like a targeted Red Rover game in which you can exercise your right and responsibility as a youth leader to call upon certain individuals that you know well and trust to live up to the high calling of entering the life of a kid.

5:1 Rituals

San Clemente Presbyterian Church is a congregation located 50 miles south of Fuller's Pasadena campus that had already embraced the importance of intergenerational relationships before FYI had even started our College Transition Project. As a result, while other churches are taking 5:1 baby steps, they are sprinting ahead. Much of their intergenerational DNA revolves around rituals, or "rites of passage," for students as they complete each grade, similar to those that can help form students' spiritual identity. (See chapter 3.)

When a student graduates from sixth grade, she is presented with a Bible with inscriptions from her parents and other friends of the family.

When that same student enters junior high, she is taken on a confirmation retreat and officially becomes a member of the San Clemente body.

At the beginning of their senior year of high school, students hike to the top of Half Dome in Yosemite with the youth pastor, the youth ministry volunteers, and the senior pastor. According to Dr. Tod Bolsinger, the senior pastor, "This tradition is so important [that] I have parents of elementary-age children telling me to keep in shape so I can take their child on this rite-of-passage hiking experience."[8]

In June of each year, the church hosts a blessing ceremony for all high school students, graduating seniors, parents, and congregation members.

Every year at this church, students experience 5:1 rituals that break down barriers between the adults' table and the kids' table.

Other 5:1 Ideas

As we've networked with and learned from other churches moving toward 5:1, we've been encouraged by their creativity. Here are a few more innovative ideas that you might want to try. Or, better yet, use them as a springboard to come up with even better ideas.

Celebrate Your Story. While serving at Saddleback Community Church, Megan Hutchinson would encourage students to share testimonies of what God was doing in their lives. The students would work with an adult volunteer to plan and write out what they wanted to share, and then invite family and friends to come to the youth group to hear the testimony.

And we also had this prayer warrior program. . . . We would sign up on a list if we wanted to have a prayer warrior as a teen, and the adults would go through and pick somebody, and they would pray for us continually and every day. We would have special dinners or time with them that we would spend together as a group, and it would be prayer warrior group time and that was really encouraging to know that someone was praying for me. . . . We felt valued and special because, I mean, they chose me off of the list . . . it's not like they drew your name out of the hat; they wanted to pray for you. . . . One of my prayer warriors I kept in touch with over my freshman and sophomore years. I emailed her quite frequently and sent cards back and forth.

—Jeanne

Parent-and-Guest Section in Your Youth Room. Follow the example of one Pennsylvania youth ministry in our Sticky Faith Learning Cohort that invites parents and other adults in the church to come and worship in the youth group meeting anytime. To make sure they feel welcome, this youth ministry has designated a special section of chairs in the back of the room just for those adults.

Retreat Guests. Similarly, invite adults from your church to join your next retreat for a morning or afternoon.

Prayer Request Exchange. Pair each high school senior with a senior adult, and invite them to share prayer requests and pray for one another. Prayer partners can write down prayer requests and then touch base periodically to see how God moves. I heard from one youth pastor who has taken these prayer pairs to a higher level. Every year, these prayer pairs participate in a bar-b-que and prayer walk so that the student-adult duos can build stickier 5:1 bonds.

Technology Tutorials. Gather high school kids with senior adults and let the teenagers teach the senior adults how to send text messages so the adults can keep in touch with their grandkids.

Youth Deacons. Consider involving a few of your more mature kids as part of the various leadership teams at your church, but make sure that one or more adult members of those teams takes those kids under their wings.

Junior/Senior Dance. Invite high school kids and senior adults together for a dance (or depending on your church tradition, maybe a banquet). Play '50s music and let the boogeying begin.

New Christian Birthday Party. Once a year, schedule a big birthday party for folks of all ages who've become Christians. Decorate with streamers and balloons, serve cake and ice cream, and invite your entire church to celebrate the "new creations" of all ages.

Child/Teenager Worship. Once a quarter, invite your teenagers to join the children's worship experience. Involve both little kids and big kids in the worship music, the announcements, and the teaching.

All-Church Camping. Get away for a weekend as an entire church and experience the beauty of God's creation together under the stars. Share stories around the campfire as you roast s'mores together.

The Role of Parents in 5:1

When I speak with a group of parents about 5:1, I often see them looking in the direction of their youth pastors, as if it's the leaders' job to build a 5:1 web for their kids. Ideally, parents assume primary responsibility for linking their kids with five or more caring adults. It's only when parents aren't able to create this web that you step in to create additional 5:1 strands.

A few months ago I met a single mom who understood that one of her responsibilities as a parent was to surround her son with loving adults, especially men who could help fill the void created by his absent father. This mom had a brilliant idea for helping her son visualize their family's sticky web. In the hallway between their bedrooms, she hung a few large collage picture frames, each of which has several openings for pictures. As her son builds a relationship with an adult—especially with a man—she takes a picture of her son with that adult. Then she places those pictures in the frames to remind them of the amazing adults surrounding their family. The

> When I go home, I go back—that's the church that I'll go to when I'm home. So whenever I'm there on Sunday, I'll catch up with all the older women that I've known since I was little, and they'll always say "hi" and they're always so excited to see me. . . . A couple of them are always so encouraging, and they'll always tell me, "Your picture is still on my fridge," and "I'm still praying for you." They always really want to know, like, "How are things?" and "What is life like there?" and they're always really encouraging.
>
> —Veronica

frames that are not yet filled remind them that there are more fantastic 5:1 relationships still to come.

A Few Final Notes

You may have noticed that many of of the 5:1 ideas above revolve around uniting teenagers and senior adults. In a typical church, both groups often feel marginalized and underappreciated. Plus, teenagers often hold a special tenderness for senior adults, and vice versa. (Remember the tight bond between 78-year-old Mr. Fredricksen and young Russell in the movie *Up*?)

Theologian Stanley Hauerwas reminds us that providing ways for senior adults to build meaningful relationships with teenagers also allows those senior adults to reach their full kingdom potential. Hauerwas convincingly argues that as Christians age, they cannot "move to Florida and leave the church to survive on its own." He continues, "For Christians, there is no 'Florida' even if they happen to live in Florida. That is, we must continue to be present to those who have made us what we are so that we can make future generations what they are called to be. Aging among Christians is not and cannot be a lost opportunity."[9] Connecting with senior adults is a great way to get your 5:1 train moving down the tracks.

Finally, those churches that are best at using 5:1 to break down the dichotomy between the "adults' table" and the "kids' table" often

use service/justice work as a springboard for intergenerational relationships. When adults and teenagers are working together to paint
a wall or feed someone who's homeless, the barriers or awkwardness
due to age quickly fall away. Our next chapter is focused on Sticky
Justice, so keep using your 5:1 lenses as you turn the page and continue reading.

sticky discussion questions

1. In what ways does your church have separate "kids' tables" and "adults' tables"? In what ways are those tables more convenient and "easier," for both kids and adults? What do you think Jesus would say about the way you tend to separate kids and adults?

2. What are the advantages of trying to surround each kid with five caring adults? What are the costs?

3. In this chapter we asked the question: "What do I do if I don't want the kids in my youth group to have the faith of the adults in my church?" What elements of the faith of the adults in your church would you want your students to emulate? What elements would you want them to avoid?

4. Given your role in your congregation, what can you do to help change your church's culture? While you may have a limited sphere of influence at your church, what changes can you suggest in your own sphere?

5. What current rituals, events, or worship services does your ministry or church offer that could be infused with a 5:1 flavor?

5

sticky justice

By not only teaching me about the Bible, but allowing me to serve and lead, high school provided me with the necessary views of Christianity to really begin to seek my relationship with Christ on my own as I set out from home.
—Jack

I became involved with high school ministry to get involved with mission/service work that they would perform. I very much enjoyed the involvement with the community and the service we did. I really did like local service work, and I developed a very deep-seated heart for giving back to the community.
—Sadie

When it was time to ask a few kids to speak at our church's Sunday evening service and share about all God had done in and through our weekend inner city trip, Demetrius was at the top of the list.

When Demetrius signed up for the trip, we weren't aware that he had a history of drug use. But on the Saturday of our mission trip, as he met men who were homeless in large part because of their own addictions, Demetrius realized that God had something better for him. That night, he wept and confessed his struggles to our entire group. He promised before God and the rest of us that he would be different when he got home.

Twenty-two hours later, I (Kara) had him sharing his story in front of our entire congregation at the Sunday night service. This time he shed no tears, but his repentance and dedication were just as genuine.

That Wednesday night, Demetrius walked into our youth room all smiles.

The same thing happened the following Sunday.

Then we didn't see Demetrius for a week.

Or a second week. Or a third.

Finally, one Sunday morning Demetrius walked back into our youth room. But this time he was cold and distant. He left as soon as youth group ended, before any of us had a chance to talk with him.

Several of us tried calling Demetrius, but he never answered and never returned our calls. I never saw him again.

In hindsight, it's clear that I made an error in asking Demetrius to share his story with the entire church so soon after such a major spiritual breakthrough. He clearly hadn't found his spiritual legs yet.

But I don't think that was the real reason Demetrius drifted from our youth ministry. He'd had a powerful justice experience, but our youth ministry didn't know how to help Demetrius move from a "mission-trip-weekend high" into a faith that would stick week in and week out.

Demetrius is not alone.

More than 2 million U.S. teens go on mission trips annually.[1] While that's something to applaud, for five out of six of them, the trips don't have much effect on their everyday lives.[2] They might be serving on weekends or over spring break, but the impact fades within days.

Sticky Findings

Our current understanding of service and justice is too narrow.

Imagine you and a few youth group kids are going out for lunch after your Sunday meeting, and you pass a man begging for money. You have a few options beyond ignoring him: You can either give him a few dollars in cash, or you can invite him into the restaurant with you and buy some food for him. Either way, you've modeled servant-hood to your students, and you've met the man's needs.

For a few hours.

These days we're meeting more and more youth leaders and students who realize that offering someone a meal can be an important first step on the path of long-term change. But that vital first step needs to be followed by other steps, like talking with him to figure out why he needed food in the first place. Or working with him to identify ways he could get his own food for weeks and months to come, and maybe even find a way off the streets altogether. This kind of long-term, systemic approach has the potential to help the man in a lasting way and to enable you and your students to turn the corner from short-term service to sustainable justice.

Justice is a biblical value and theme.

Maybe you're like one youth worker who recently told me that his church "freaks out" when he says the word *justice.* He says that term seems to trigger one of two images in his church members' minds: either radical druggie hippies from the 1960s or "liberal" believers who talk more about freedom and rights than Jesus or salvation.

I responded, "Then your church hasn't read the Bible. The Bible talks about justice as one of God's core attributes, and it's a word that we have to reclaim."

Just a smattering of Scripture passages reveals God's deep concern for justice:

- Deuteronomy 16:20—"Follow **justice** and **justice** alone, so that you may live and possess the land the LORD your God is giving you."
- Deuteronomy 27:19—"Cursed is anyone who withholds **justice** from the foreigner, the fatherless or the widow."
- Psalm 7:6—"Arise, LORD, in your anger; rise up against the rage of my enemies. Awake, my God; decree **justice**."
- Psalm 103:6—"The Lord works righteousness and **justice** for all the oppressed."

- Psalm 106:3—"Blessed are those who act **justly**, who always do what is right."
- Isaiah 28:17—"I will make **justice** the measuring line and righteousness the plumb line."
- Isaiah 61:8—"For I, the LORD, love **justice**."
- Jeremiah 9:24—"But let the one who boasts boast about this: that they have the understanding to know me, that I am the LORD, who exercises kindness, **justice** and righteousness on earth, for in these I delight."
- Amos 5:24—"But let **justice** roll on like a river, righteousness like a never-failing stream!"
- Micah 6:8—"He has shown you, O mortal, what is good. And what does the LORD require of you? To act **justly** and to love mercy and to walk humbly with your God."
- Matthew 12:18—"Here is my servant whom I have chosen, the one I love, in whom I delight; I will put my Spirit on him, and he will proclaim **justice** to the nations."
- Luke 18:7—"And will not God bring about **justice** for his chosen ones, who cry out to him day and night? Will he keep putting them off?"

Kingdom justice meets all sorts of needs.

Another word in Scripture that's closely linked with the term *justice* is *shalom* (pronounced "Shuh-LOME"). We tend to think of *shalom* as "peace"—as in an individual's subjective sense of peace ("I feel peace about meeting my upcoming deadline") or the absence of violence and physical conflict ("We are praying for peace in the Middle East").

Those are both accurate, but like our understanding of justice, our understanding of *shalom* is too small. In describing *shalom* and its relationship to justice, Dr. Nicholas Wolterstorff, professor of philosophical theology at Yale University, writes:

The state of shalom *is the state of flourishing in all dimensions of one's existence: in one's relation to God, in one's relation to one's fel-*

low human beings, in one's relation to nature, and in one's relation to oneself. Evidently justice has something to do with the fact that God's love for each and every one of God's human creatures takes the form of God desiring the shalom of each and every one.[3]

Far more than just a warm and fuzzy feeling, God's *shalom* means we right wrongs around us—both locally and globally—so that all can experience the holistic flourishing that God intends.

Kids want to be involved in service and justice work.

Here's some good news: The students we surveyed have told us they want to extend God's *shalom* to the least, the last, and the lost. We asked graduating high school seniors what they wished they'd had more of in youth group. Of the 13 options we provided, their number one answer was "time for deep conversation"—the kind of deep conversation we will discuss more in chapter 7, "Sticky Youth Groups."

Second was mission trips.

Third was service projects.

Last was games. (Granted, a survey of seventh grade boys may have yielded a different hierarchy.)

Along a similar vein, 60 percent of the seniors we surveyed were motivated to come to youth group because of the ways youth group has helped them learn to serve. Youth ministries struggling to retain upperclassmen—in other words, most youth ministries—would be wise to pay attention to this Sticky Finding.

Even MTV is realizing that justice is "in" with kids and young adults. While MTV continues to air shows that elevate decadence (like *My Super Sweet 16* and *MTV Cribs),* the network is also planning to broadcast reality TV shows that showcase kids traveling across the country and making wishes come true for deserving locals who face debilitating diseases or are trapped in poverty.[4] Wouldn't it be great if someday MTV devoted an entire show to kids of faith engaged in Sticky Justice?

If kids aren't diving into service, it might be because we aren't asking them to do so.

Periodically a youth leader will tell me his kids don't seem all that interested in justice work. Perhaps part of the problem is that we aren't doing a very good job of inviting students to dive into kingdom service.

One study indicates that 93 percent of adolescents who were asked to volunteer by someone close to them, did volunteer. In contrast, only 24 percent of those who volunteered did not have someone close to them extend such a personal invitation.[5] So maybe instead of just sending out an email or text to a large group of students or coming up with a creative video announcement, we need to pick up the phone or ask individual students face-to-face if they'd like to join us on our justice journey.

Service and justice work—as we currently do them—are not sticking like we'd hope.

Recent research conducted by two friends and colleagues from other schools, Dr. Robert Priest from Trinity Evangelical Divinity School and Dr. Kurt Ver Beek from Calvin College, suggests that our current service experiences might not be producing the spiritual and relational "bang" we hope for—at least not in the long term. For example:

- The explosive growth in the number of short-term mission trips among both kids and adults has *not* translated into similarly explosive growth in the number of career missionaries.
- It's not clear whether participation in service trips causes participants to give more money to alleviate poverty once they return to life as usual.
- Service trips do not seem to reduce participants' tendencies toward materialism.[6]

To paraphrase the *Field of Dreams* mantra: If we send them, they will grow . . .

Maybe.

Service is stickier when it hits close to home.

A few years ago, MTV conducted a nationwide survey focused on understanding how and why U.S. youth are already active in social causes.[7] Here's what MTV found:

> • The top five reasons kids are not involved are:
>   1. It's just not for me (18 percent).
>   2. I like to hang out with friends (15 percent).
>   3. I don't have enough time (14 percent).
>   4. I don't know how to get started (14 percent).
>   5. I want to see concrete results (8 percent).
> • Sixty-two percent say the issues that matter most to them are those that have touched them or someone they know.
> • Seventy percent of kids involved in activism report that their parents' encouragement played a major factor in their choice to get involved.
> • The top two factors that would motivate kids to be more involved are:
>   1. If they could do the activity with their friends
>   2. If they had more time to volunteer or more convenient volunteer activities[8]

As we think about our role in creating space for kids to experience sticky service, one theme emerges from the MTV findings: Justice will be stickier when it hits kids close to home. It needs to be in the home *literally* as we invite parents to exemplify, encourage, and participate with their own kids in righting wrongs around them. It needs to hit close to home *thematically* as we help kids understand how particular injustices relate to their lives. It needs to hit home *personally* as we expose our kids to actual people who have been oppressed, thereby giving injustice a face and a name. And justice ministry needs to hit home *relationally* as we help kids serve others in partnership with their friends.

Sticky Faith Made Practical

Service or justice work is more likely to stick when it's not an event but a process.

So our research indicates the good news that kids want to serve and that for some kids, service plays a significant part in their growing faith. But as we've seen, the bad news is that we're falling far short of the fruit we could be yielding from the justice vine.

Over the past few years, we at FYI, in collaboration with Dr. Dave Livermore of the Global Learning Center at Grand Rapids Theological Seminary and Dr. Terry Linhart of Bethel College (Indiana), have convened two summits of experts in short-term missions for honest discussions about what research says we are—and are not—accomplishing through our mission work.[9] One theme repeatedly emerges: We need to do a better job of walking with students before, during, and after their mission experiences.[10]

Let's be honest. Our "preparation" as youth workers before the typical short-term mission trip usually consists of what I call "M&Ms": Money and Medical releases. Our "reflection" during the trip boils down to a few minutes of prayer requests at the end of the day before team members tumble into their beds, exhausted. And our "debrief" after we get home is little more than organizing the media show and the testimonies to share in "big church."

If we want students' justice work and their faith to stick, we need a completely different time frame for our service. Perhaps instead of viewing a weekend trip to work with homeless people in the inner city as a three-day commitment, we need to view it as a three-month process. Instead of looking at a week in Guatemala as seven days, we need to think of it as a seven-month journey.

The Before/During/After Model

So what do youth ministries do with those extra weeks before and after the service experience? As a result of our summits, our surveys of kids, and our interviews with youth workers, we at FYI recommend an experiential education framework originally proposed by Laura Joplin[11] and later modified and tested by Dr. Terry Linhart[12] on youth mission trips.

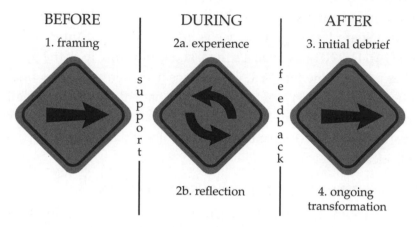

Figure 5.1 The Before/During/After Model[13]

Step 1. BEFORE: FRAMING

A sticky service or justice experience starts when we help students FRAME the sometimes mind-blowing and other times menial experiences that await them. Getting ready for a mission experience involves much more than just helping kids raise money, learn a drama, or know what to pack. Our job as leaders is to facilitate a series of gatherings and events ahead of time that prepares students emotionally, mentally, spiritually, and relationally for what they'll face.

Step 2. DURING: EXPERIENCE AND REFLECTION

The main component in students' learning during their actual service is the cycle of EXPERIENCE AND REFLECTION. The constant barrage of experiences on a typical service adventure comes so fast and furious that kids often feel as if they're sprinting through a museum, barely viewing its masterpieces out of the corners of their eyes. As adult leaders, our job is to give space for students to catch their breath and ask questions to help decipher the sticky meaning behind their observations, thoughts, and feelings.

Step 3: AFTER: INITIAL DEBRIEF

At the end of our justice work, as students' minds and the ministry's minivans are heading home, we've now entered the third step of INITIAL DEBRIEF. Maybe it's the last day of your trip as the group takes a bit of time for R&R. Or perhaps it's when the group hits a coffee shop together right after visiting patients at the local children's hospital. Either way, the goal is to gather the team together after the "work" is completed to start thinking about what you hope will stick long term.

Step 4: AFTER: ONGOING TRANSFORMATION

If most youth groups lack an effective pre-service framing time, even more fail to give proper attention to ONGOING TRANSFOR-MATION after the experience. Two realities fight against effective learning transfer. First, most of the significant growth in a service experience takes place in an environment very different from students' home communities. Second, the students themselves don't know how to translate the learning to their own lives. That's why we adults need to help them connect the dots between having lunch with a homeless man in Baltimore and having lunch with a new kid in their school cafeteria one week (or even one day) later.

Through it all: SUPPORT and FEEDBACK

To facilitate the experience-and-reflection cycle, our discussions and activities need to be surrounded by walls of SUPPORT and FEED-BACK. While these two expressions of care are vital throughout the process, their importance peaks during the time you're actually serving. It's crucial to take the time to listen to students' felt needs, as well as dig deeper to some of their underlying real needs, so we can offer perspective to students whose heads might be spinning due to new experiences and observations.

The Extra Time Pays Off

Two months ago, I (Kara) was part of a weekend mission trip to inner city Los Angeles along with teenagers from my church. I can't even count how many inner city trips I've participated in with teenagers. But this trip was different. And better.

We had a surprise for the students: The weekend was actually a poverty simulation. We'd told their parents ahead of time, but to the students' shock, they showed up on Friday night and were told they had to surrender all of their possessions. They could keep two items, and their sleeping bags counted as one of them. So most everyone kept a sleeping bag, and then each person chose one toiletry item. One girl kept her toothpaste, another her toothbrush, and then they shared. It made for interesting community.

Next, the kids relinquished the clothes off their backs and chose clothes from Goodwill to wear instead.

The students slept outside until 4:30 a.m. on Saturday, at which point they were woken up by the adult leaders because of an ordinance in Los Angeles that prohibits sleeping outside after sunrise.

Each person's breakfast consisted of one-half of a saltine cracker and a few sips of lemonade.

They did manual labor that Saturday morning, cleaning bathrooms and kitchens in the community.

By the time lunch rolled around, they were tired, grimy, and hungry. The only way for them to get lunch was to beg for money (one of the many reasons I was glad we'd obtained parents' permission for the poverty simulation).

The Staples Center (home of the Los Angeles Lakers and Kings) and the Los Angeles Convention Center were just a 10-minute walk from Pico Union, the lower income community in which our group was staying. My group of four students, plus myself and another leader, decided to walk there and ask strangers for money. Interestingly, one girl in my group told me that several of her friends had gone to see Britney Spears in concert at the Staples Center the night before. In fact, they took a limo to the show. Now this girl was standing outside that same Staples Center, wearing clothes from Goodwill, asking people for food money. The contrast couldn't have been more stark.

The girls and guys in the group could legitimately approach strangers and say they hadn't eaten that day. After about 45 minutes, our group had $2.25.

Just over two dollars wouldn't normally be enough to feed two hungry adults and four hungry teenagers, but there was a 99 Cent Store in Pico Union. We walked there and used our $2.25 to purchase a loaf of bread and a jar of peanut butter. We had no knife, so I used the wax paper covering on top of the peanut butter as a makeshift knife.

As we sat on the dirty sidewalk, getting peanut butter all over ourselves and our clothes, our kids kept repeating, "These are the best peanut butter sandwiches *ever.*"

Later that day as the entire group debriefed with the local leader hosting us, he said they have high school and college groups experience this poverty simulation almost every weekend. Apparently, ours was the first group of high school students who didn't cry when their stuff was confiscated.

I love the kids at our church, but I don't think of them as particularly tough. Afterward I asked our youth pastor why he thought the students did so well. His answer was immediate and simple, "We trained them ahead of time." It was the pre-service training meetings focused on what it's like to experience poverty that helped them dive in immediately instead of rejecting or resenting the justice challenge facing them.

Sticky Causes

The youth workers I know who are best at engaging kids in Sticky Justice are those who connect kids with sticky causes—causes the kids can identify with personally.

A couple of years ago, I was stunned by a *New York Times* article profiling segregated high school proms.[14] I had no idea such proms still existed, but at a few public schools in Georgia and Tennessee that offer only one "official" prom, parents have banded together to offer an unofficial "white" prom and a "black" prom. (By the way, did you catch that the *parents* are the ones behind these segregated proms?)

I'm not sure if I'm more mad or sad. But I do know this: If I were a youth worker in these areas, I'd be talking about this close-to-home injustice with students, brainstorming ways we could right this wrong.

One youth worker has found that female students in her youth ministry have a special connection with victims of sex trafficking.

Another has found that his students' bumpy academic road during high school has burdened them to tutor and mentor elementary school kids.

What is it that strikes close to home for your students? If you don't have an answer to that question, get one by asking your kids.

Sticky, Ongoing Relationships

Viewing justice as a sticky Before/During/After process also allows you and your students to develop real and ongoing relationships with the people who host you for mission experiences. We stumbled onto the power of long-term connections at our church. When I (Kara) was college pastor, we took 30 college students to Tijuana for the weekend to build a house. That same weekend, to our total surprise, an adult class from our church was just a tenth of a mile away, working with the same organization on a different house. It was marvelous for our students to see adults engaged in kingdom work and vice versa.

Once our group returned to Pasadena, I started dreaming with our missions pastor about how we could develop justice work that was truly transformative. The organization we were working with had been sending five different classes from our church all over Tijuana. Each class went down a few times per year, so members of our church were building 10 houses annually, but the houses were miles from one another.

We asked the host organization if we could focus our

congregation's efforts on one community in Tijuana—Cumbres. So they started sending all of our classes to Cumbres. Every time we went, we were able to visit people living in the houses that we and other members of our church had partnered with the locals to build. We saw the tangible difference those houses were making for the broader community. The folks in Cumbres became our friends, and we stayed in touch between trips through letters and phone calls.

Having built real, ongoing relationships with the folks in Cumbres, we decided to take it up a notch. We and the locals had a God-sized dream of launching a church in Cumbres. Our church in California offered to fund the first two years of a full-time salary for Sergio, a resident of Cumbres, so he could become the pastor of that congregation. Then we cut our support in half for the next two years, to help the church transition to funding its own leadership on the path toward long-term sustainability. At the end of four years, the people of Cumbres had their own church with their own pastor—a pastor whom they were funding 100 percent.

We are still in contact with the folks in Cumbres, but we don't go down as often anymore. Cumbres has a vibrant church, and our relationship has evolved.

That's justice that sticks.

Kids' Sticky Creativity

At a youth ministry conference last year, I met Matthew Deprez, the Now Generation pastor at Frontline Community Church in Grand Rapids, Michigan. Since then we've kept in touch by email and phone, sharing ideas about Sticky Faith. Matthew's experience with the youth of his church captures much of what we've learned in our Sticky Faith research about justice. It also captures the amazing potential of students' creativity to make a difference in someone else's life.

In October 2009, a team from the church did a short-term mission trip in Port au Prince, Haiti. In Port au Prince, the team met Kelencia, a two-year-old who wore size-one diapers. The team was told that Kelencia had a hole in her heart, and Haitian doctors reported that if she didn't have surgery, there was a very good chance she would die within the year. The team called hospitals all over Michigan, and a hospital in Ann Arbor agreed to do the $100,000 surgery for free. All the church had to do was raise a few thousand dollars for a round-trip plane ticket and other expenses like a visa, clothing, and food for Kelencia while she was in the United States.

The church's teenagers volunteered to raise the funds. Working in small groups, the kids poured every ounce of their God-given creativity into their fundraising. One group of high school girls learned how to knit and spent two straight weekends knitting washcloths and dish towels, which they then sold, raising $200.

Another group of kids bought a bunch of jelly beans and created a poem based on the different colored jelly beans and how they related to Scripture. They packaged them in small plastic bags with the poem and Kelencia's story attached, and sold them to friends, family, and complete strangers. They made $250.

Several youth raised more than $300 by going door-to-door collecting cans on a freezing December Saturday. Another student invited his family members to write checks directly to the "Kelencia Project" rather than giving him Christmas gifts. And still another contributed $200 of her Christmas money, saying Kelencia needed the money more than she did.

In all, the youth raised $2,200, more than enough to cover the cost of Kelencia's travel and other expenses. Early in January, the entire church celebrated the exciting news that Kelencia would be flying to Michigan later that year for her life-saving surgery.

But three days after the celebration, on January 12, 2010, the major earthquake hit Haiti. A day later, the church received a phone call and news that Kelencia's entire town was leveled, and she didn't survive.

Matthew described in an email what that experience was like for the teenagers. "That night we made an announcement to the kids who had just raised all this money for her. Words can't describe what that night was like. Students wept for hours. It was horrible."

But one student's response was a little different. Ian went to Matthew and asked, "Are you 100 percent sure that Kelencia is dead?"

Matthew's honest answer was, "No, but we are 99 percent sure."

Ian replied, "I won't believe it until it's 100 percent. I am hanging on to that one percent."

Ian's optimism was well founded. Twenty-four hours later, the church received another phone call from Haiti saying that Kelencia was alive, and she barely had a scratch on her.

Four months later, Ian and his dad were among the members of the church who traveled to the Haitian orphanage and met Kelencia face-to-face. Ian's time with Kelencia and the other children at the orphanage strengthened his interest in studying to be a teacher. And a few months after that, Kelencia traveled to the United States for the surgery that saved her life.

> For more stories and ideas from youth workers around the country who are engaging kids in service and justice, or to share your own story, visit the Deep Justice Stories page at www.fulleryouthinstitute.org.

Recently I presented our research findings about Sticky Justice at a conference for youth workers and high school kids. During my seminar, we talked together about how our youth ministries could tangibly help folks who are homeless in our communities.

One youth worker shared his frustration with a city ordinance that prohibits anyone from giving food or clothing to folks who are homeless. At this point, a teenager in the seminar raised his hand and asked, "How about if you invite the homeless to come and eat with you? There's no law against that, is there?"

I smiled and asked, "How old are you?"

"Thirteen."

Priceless. I love the creativity of teenagers when it comes to justice. They are sticking with it.

sticky discussion questions

1. How would you define the difference between *service* and *justice*?

2. What examples have you seen of service experiences not producing the spiritual "bang for the buck" you hoped for and expected? Why do you think they've fallen short?

3. Think about your next service experience. What could you do before the event to help prepare kids for what they will face? What could you do afterward? If you had to drop other ministry events to make space in your calendar, what would you drop?

4. Think about a few kids in your ministry. How can you help unleash their creativity to see God's kingdom justice come on earth as it is in heaven? As their youth leader, what will you need to do differently?

6

sticky family relationships

I chose the career that I am in now, speech language pathology, because my dad sat me down so much and looked at what I love to do, and he let me just sit down and spill all my thoughts. Through those conversations I would realize, "Oh, wow, I'd really love to do this" or "I'm actually really good at this" . . . because of that, this field that I get to work in now is the most fulfilling and the most wonderful field to be in.
—Robyn

They were probably the biggest influence. And I know that if my parents hadn't shown me through example what it was to be a Christian, I probably would have had a very difficult time doing it.
—Dale

Especially in high school, they were teaching me how to make good decisions and kind of guiding me in that, but really not controlling what I did as much as, "Let's talk through how to make a good godly decision and how you seek God's will for things."
—Annika

"Kara, I need to ask for your forgiveness."

I couldn't think of anything that Linda, a single mom of two teenagers who were both part of our youth ministry, had done wrong, so

I was surprised she felt the need to ask for my forgiveness. The last year had been a roller coaster for Linda, full of the highs of watching her son sprint forward spiritually, as well as the lows of her daughter's spiritual stumbles. Seventeen-year-old Kimberly had become pregnant and had quickly made the choice to have an abortion. This double blow left Linda reeling.

Linda began to cry as she confessed to me, "For over a year, I've been mad at you for what happened to Kimberly. I've blamed you and held you responsible."

Gulp.

I had no idea Linda blamed me for her daughter's choices.

In response to Linda's tearful confession, I hugged her and told her that I forgave her and that I understood. I assured her that it is normal for parents navigating storms with their kids to wish that their youth leader could be some sort of all-powerful shelter. When we can't, parents' disappointment can turn to frustration and even blame.

Yet as I thought about Linda over the next few days, I became more and more angry. Not at Linda, but at a church culture that had allowed parents to outsource the development of their kids to me as the youth leader.

I saw Kimberly three hours per week for four years of her life—at most. During those same three hours, I also saw a few hundred other teenagers. How could anyone think that I was somehow more responsible for Kimberly than her mom, someone who saw Kimberly every day for the first 17 years of her life?

Sticky Findings

Read Carefully: Parents are usually the most important influence in their kids' lives.

Not only is it exhausting to be responsible for every kid's Sticky Faith (or lack thereof), but it's not very effective. While I believe in the power of adult mentoring (after all, I'm a weekly small group leader at my church), it's difficult to find a Sticky Faith factor that is more significant than students' parents.

Based on his nationwide telephone survey of more than 3 thousand teens and their parents, as well as 267 in-depth interviews, sociologist Dr. Christian Smith from the University of Notre Dame concluded: "Most teenagers and their parents may not realize it, but a lot of research in the sociology of religion suggests that the most important social influence in shaping young people's religious lives is the religious life modeled and taught to them by their parents."[1]

Christian Smith put it even more simply and succinctly while speaking as part of a panel with Chap Clark and me: "When it comes to kids' faith, parents get what they are."[2]

Of course there are exceptions. Your faith may be vastly different from the faith of your parents. Plus, I've met plenty of dedicated Christian parents whose kids end up all over the faith spectrum. But parents are more than an initial launch pad for their kids' journey; they continue to shape them as an ongoing companion and guide.

Most parents miss out on the opportunity to talk about faith with their kids.

At Fuller Seminary, we have great respect and affection for the Search Institute, a fellow research center devoted to helping families, schools, and kids make the world a better place for kids. According to the Search Institute's nationwide study of 11,000 teenagers from 561 congregations across 6 denominations, 12 percent of youth have a regular dialogue with their mom on faith/life issues.[3] In other words, one out of eight kids talks with Mom about faith.

It's far lower for dads. One out of twenty, or 5 percent, of kids have regular faith/life conversations with Dad.

> Even though my mother was actually working at the church for a while as the music minister . . . we didn't talk about faith at home. Still don't talk about it at home.
>
> —Anthony

One additional interesting statistic: Approximately 9 percent of teenagers engage in regular reading of the Bible and devotions with their families. So not even one out of ten teenagers looks at Scripture with their parents. When it comes to matters of faith, mum's usually the word at home.

The best discussions about faith happen when parents don't just ask questions, but also share their own experiences.

The relatively small percentage of parents who *do* talk with their kids about faith tend to default to asking their kids questions.

What did you talk about in church today?

How was youth group?

What did you think of the sermon?

Depending on the personality and mood of the kid, responses usually range from grunts to "the usual." Not very satisfying for the parent or the kid.

Our research shows that asking these questions can pay off. But what is vital to Sticky Faith is that parents also *share about their own faith.*

In other words, parents shouldn't merely interview their kids; they need to *discuss their own faith journeys,* including both ups and downs.

When I talk with groups of parents about the fruit that comes from sharing about their faith with their kids, eventually one or more parents will chime in that they believe living out their faith in front of their kids is more important than merely talking about it.

I'll quickly concede that who we are as parents has a much greater impact than what we say. If I had to choose between living out my faith and talking about my faith around my own kids, I'd choose the former every time.

But I don't have to choose. And neither do the parents in your ministry. Parents can do both.[4]

Unfortunately, Christian parents are less likely than other parents to talk about tricky subjects with their kids.

Perhaps one reason these conversations aren't happening in the home is because parents don't know how (or maybe they are afraid or too busy) to talk about certain issues that might be raised. It's almost like all parents are given the same list of topics to avoid discussing with their kids.

Sex is certainly on that list. Two different sets of data indicate that the more important religion (not just Christianity, but also other religions) is to parents, the more difficult it is for those same parents to talk with their kids about sex.[5]

I find that both disappointing and incredibly ironic. We followers of Christ should be at the front of the line to talk with kids about sex because we know that sex, when done right, is really right. Somehow with sex (and I would surmise other controversial topics), families have been robbed of healthy, balanced, scripturally guided conversations—the type of conversations that foster Sticky Faith.

Sticky Faith Made Practical

I'm guessing that few youth workers would disagree with the data suggesting that parents are generally the most significant influence on kids. You already know parents will almost always have a larger impact on their kids than you can as a youth worker. But is that knowledge translating to your ministry calendar? How much of your time do you devote to helping parents develop Sticky Faith in their kids? If you're like most youth workers, it's probably less than 10 percent.

Maybe 10 percent is all you can give . . .

Or, maybe you could give more than 10 percent, but you're not sure what to do with that time . . .

If you're wondering how to maximize the impact of the time you spend helping parents develop Sticky Families, our research and conversations with youth leaders and parents nationwide reveals three points of leverage.

> In chapter 9, we will further highlight the power of story in bringing about Sticky Faith changes.

Leverage Point 1: Plant the Sticky Faith Vision
Through Stories of Other Families

You may or may not be a parent yourself. And even though the average age of youth leaders is on the rise, if you do have kids, they may not yet be teenagers. As one Fuller colleague kidded me, "Kara, you haven't gone to the jail of parenting teenagers yet."

True, I haven't, but one of the great benefits of my experience in youth ministry is the hundreds of families I have closely observed. Regardless of your age or family situation, one of the best ways to leverage your time with parents is to share the Sticky Faith stories of other innovative parents—either stories of parents in your ministry or stories of parents that have emerged from our research.

Share stories that motivate parents to make space and time for quality conversations.

Even though my oldest child is only 11, my parenting is different every day because of our Sticky Faith research. At the very top of the long list of what I've learned is that my husband and I need to make space and time for quality conversations with our kids.

Note that I didn't say we have to hope that space emerges.

I said we have to "make" the space.

In the midst of preparing dinner, writing emails, and thinking about tomorrow's meetings (usually all at once), I find it very challenging to make time to really talk with my kids. I fail all the time. But even then, our research has made me more determined than ever to try, try again.

Our family has found it helpful to try to carve out time each week to be together—time we call "Powell Time."

> I can remember incredible conversations with my parents where we're learning from each other, where they're sharing with me why they believe what they believe and then me sharing what I believed, and just an opportunity for growth for both of us, for both my parents and myself.
>
> —Peter

120

Sometimes all five of us do something together; but most of the time, Dave takes one or two of our kids and I take the other(s). We mix it up each week so that both Dave and I get one-on-one (or one-on-two) time with each kid. For our kids, that time is like gold.

There are two goals for Powell Time: to have fun and to talk. Usually it's cheap fun, like playing tennis or going on a hike or making cookies. And then we sit and talk with each other, usually over frozen yogurt or a blended juice drink. We even have special notebooks for these conversations, notebooks our kids picked out for themselves at our first Powell Time. The parent starts the conversation asking Nathan, Krista, or Jessica questions and capturing their answers in their journals.

We tend to ask questions like: What would your friends say they like about you?

What do you wish was different about our family?

Do you think our family is too busy, not busy enough, or just right?

What's your idea of the best day ever?

Because of what we've learned about Sticky Faith, we also give our kids a chance to ask *us* questions, and we write down our own answers. Their questions can be pretty amusing:

What's your favorite dessert?

What do you do all day at Fuller?

What could we do during our next Powell Time?

Our kids are young, but we're trying to plant honest conversation into the DNA of our relationship.

During the course of our research, our FYI team has been continually impressed with parents' creativity in planting that same DNA in their own families. Cheryl talked with one dad who would take each of his four daughters out for a one-on-one breakfast date every week. Yes, that's four breakfast dates every week. And he did that with them throughout middle school and high school.

A year ago I met Eileen, a mother of two teenagers who had decided to sit and watch TV with her kids when they had the TV on, but she would hold the remote. During or after scenes that showed something related to sex, drugs, or alcohol—or anything controversial or provocative, for that matter—Eileen would hit the pause button, ask her kids questions, and share her own thoughts. At times Eileen finds the best question to ask her kids is simply, "What should that character have done?"

I asked Eileen if her kids ever roll their eyes at her questions and commentary. "Sure, at times they do. But sometimes we get into good conversations. And every once in a while, they later parrot back to me something I've said. Like all parents, I'm planting seeds."

A successful business leader I met focuses his conversational seed-planting on one of his major values: wisdom. Many of his conversations with his three daughters revolve around helping them make better decisions. Over dinner or as he's driving his girls to soccer practice, he talks to his daughters about their days, keeping an ear tuned to the decisions they made throughout the day—decisions ranging from how they spent their time to how they interacted with friends. He asks them why they made the decisions they did and if they would make the same decision again. He also shares with his girls about both the good and not-so-good decisions he has made. He and his wife steer conversations in this direction because of their shared goal of teaching their kids to be independent thinkers.

> I feel like the number one way that my parents have influenced me is by showing me a strong Christ-based marriage . . . where they've been a team and they have worked through stuff together. And I've learned so much through that.
>
> —Hayley

The intentional effort, time, and thought parents must pour into conversations with their kids doesn't end when the kids graduate from high school. Recently I spoke with Rowena, whose son is a college freshman living on a university campus 30 minutes from their home. When Rowena calls his cell phone, he's often headed to class or on his way to lunch and has little time to talk. His occasional moodiness doesn't help.

But he does need regular haircuts. He likes the barber who cut his hair while he was in high school, but he doesn't have a car at school to drive himself back home. So this busy mom of three makes an effort every month to pick up her son at school, take him for a haircut, and then drive him back.

At first her husband objected, "This is silly. He's a college student. He can get his own haircut."

But then Rowena explained that it wasn't about the haircut. It was about the 30-minute car rides they shared going to and from the barber—just the two of them.

It is during those car rides that she gets the best glimpse of how her son is doing. It was during a car ride that he mentioned the encouraging news that he had started attending the school's chapter of Campus Crusade for Christ. He never would have mentioned that during their short phone calls, but the 30-minute car rides give her son time to unpack his life.

Help parents talk about their own Sticky Faith.
Throughout this Sticky Faith research process, I've realized so many errors I've made as a parent. Take our family devotions. We try to have family devotions every weekend. Lest you be under any illusions, they last less than 10 minutes—and if it's an extra busy weekend or if a really good Charger game is on TV, they may not happen at all.

Since we tend to do family devotions on Sundays, we used to ask our kids one at a time what they talked about in church that day. Then we'd read and discuss a passage of Scripture (usually a story), share prayer requests, and pray for one another.

Where did we go wrong? We never shared what *we* had learned in church. We were *interviewing* our kids instead of having a *mutual conversation* with them. Now when we ask our kids to share about what they learned in church, we talk about what we learned too.

There is no question that it's valuable for parents to ask their kids questions about their lives and faith. But based on our research, we urge parents to make sure they are answering those questions also.

On nights when our family has dinner together, we have a tradition of sharing our "highs" and "lows" of the day. Because of what we've learned about Sticky Faith, we've added a third question: *How did you see God at work today?*

The first time we added that question to our conversation, our seven-year-old said quickly, "But I can't answer that question."

"Why not?" I asked.

"Because I don't have a job."

When she heard the question, "How did you see God *at work* today?" she thought she was supposed to answer how she saw God *at her job.* Once we explained that we meant, "How did you see God *working* today?" she realized she could be part of the discussion.

Often our kids don't have an answer to that question, and that's okay. In fact, as important as the kids answering that question is that they hear Dave and me answer that question every day.

> So many kids don't know when and how their parents started following Christ. Most kids love hearing about when their parents met, when they fell in love, and what their wedding day was like. Why don't parents share the same details about their faith story? Maybe one of your first Sticky Faith steps as a youth leader is to encourage parents to share with their kids how they became a Christian. What led them down that path? What did it feel like? What surprised them about those early days as a believer?

If the parents of your teenagers haven't already been talking about their faith, trying to ask specific questions will likely feel awkward and forced. Encourage parents who are just getting started to try asking their kids a simple question that a host of parents have found helpful: *How can I be praying for you?* Whether it's in person or by text, email, or phone, many parents find the answers their kids give to that question provide a valuable window into their lives.

I've met one parent who takes her kids' prayer requests a step further. Periodically, she asks both of her sons (one is in college, the other in high school) to write down how they'd like her to pray for them. She makes a copy of these prayer requests and gives the originals back to her sons. When they look at those lists later, they are reminded that their mom is praying for them every day.

One dad told me his goal was simply to mention God in at least one conversation with his kids every day. Simple. But Sticky.

Leverage Point 2: Help Parents Learn to Listen and Ask Questions Instead of Lecturing

Throughout our research process, parents have repeatedly told us the best conversations with their kids occur in the midst of everyday life—when they are in the minivan together after hockey practice, or when their kid is stressed over finding a prom date. Those times of crisis or debrief of the day's events are often the best springboards for deeper conversation.

How can you as a youth worker help parents leverage these everyday opportunities? Our best answer is that you can train them to listen and ask questions instead of lecturing.

Parents lecturing kids doesn't work.

The well-known philosopher Dallas Willard writes, "But now let us try out a subversive thought. Suppose our failures occur, not in spite of what we are doing, but precisely because of it."[6] Maybe one of the main reasons parents struggle to communicate with their kids is because they are trying to communicate by lecturing.

The most important Sticky Faith communication advice you can give parents is this: *Never explain something to your kid if you can ask a question instead.*

Why is this so important? Picture a teenager and her parents talking about premarital sex. Does the kid know what her parents think about it? Does the kid know what her parents want her to say about it? Odds are good that the answer to both questions is yes.

Because they already know both what their parents think and what the parents want them to say, kids will likely close their minds as soon as parents open their mouths. One noted psychologist who is also a dad recently relayed the story of talking to his 16-year-old son about a behavior the dad felt should be changed. After the dad's long and well-reasoned list of reasons the son should change, the son shrugged and said, "Are you done yet?" Note that the question was "Are *you* done yet?" not "Are *we* done yet?"

Help parents learn how to ask questions rather than lecture their teenagers. During one-on-one conversations or regularly scheduled training meetings with parents, you can . . .

- Role-play how to handle tough subjects.
- Help parents think of questions that will help kids not be defensive.
- Convene parents to share both horror stories of conversations gone bad as well as encouraging stories of conversations that went well.

The more parents can plan ahead and practice with you, the more likely it is that their later conversations with their kids will stick.

Set up parents to succeed in their conversations.
Our Sticky Faith research team has gleaned a host of practical ways you as a youth worker can help parents succeed in their conversations with kids:

Give parents regular updates on youth culture. Parents are eager for resources that will help them better understand and relate to their kids. You can email monthly tips or resources to parents that will both alleviate their anxieties about their kids' behavior and equip them to talk more effectively with their kids.

For more free resources that are specially geared for parents, visit www.stickyfaith.org or the Center for Parent and Youth Understanding at www.cpyu.org.

Debrief big events with parents in person. Tim Nielson, the youth pastor at Grace Chapel in Denver, decided he wanted to help his parents process their kids' experiences on the annual winter youth retreat. So he left the retreat early to meet with the parents at his church an hour before the kids arrived. He took this hour to share the spiritual highlights of the weekend and give parents questions they could ask their kids related to the Scriptures covered during the retreat. As a bonus, since parents showed up an hour early, Tim and his team didn't have to wait around for parents who were late to pick up their kids.

Email debriefs as the second-best option. It's not always feasible for you to leave a major event early in order to debrief with parents. (For example, if you're driving the church bus, it's best not to delegate that to one of the kids.) If you don't have a chance to meet in person with parents, send them a simple debrief sheet on the day you get back that includes a summary of what God seems to be doing and a few questions they can ask their kids.

Encourage parents to check in with you. The more parents know what's happening in their kids' lives, the better their conversations. Without betraying any kids' confidences, encourage parents to touch base with you periodically so you can share how you see God working in their kid, as well as any concerns you might have.

Take initiative with parents yourself. Often the only time parents hear from youth workers is when their kid is causing problems. Build time into your calendar to call parents or send them emails letting them know what's happening with their kids, empowering them to ask better questions as they talk with their kids. After all, if schools can arrange a 20-minute parent-teacher conference for each kid every year, why can't churches?

Model good conversations when you have dinner with families. Many youth leaders have shared how beneficial they find it to have dinner with kids and their families. Take advantage of the time around the table to model good conversation by asking everyone to share a "high" and "low" of the day, or to talk about one new thing each person is learning about God. Doing this with you might make it easier for the family to do the same thing the next night when you're not there.

Have parents share their testimonies with your ministry. One Los Angeles youth leader regularly invites parents of her kids to share their personal testimonies with the entire youth ministry. Not only does that make it more likely that a parent may have deeper conversations with his or her own kid afterward, but it also motivates other kids to go a bit deeper with their parents.

How do I help parents whose kids don't want to talk to them?

When I share with parents the importance of having good conversations with their kids, often one of them will sheepishly raise a hand and ask, "What if your kid doesn't want to talk to you?"

All teenagers go through seasons when they don't want to talk to their parents. What varies is the length and intensity of the season. The longer and more intense the season, the more creative parents need to be.

One mom desperately wanted to have meaningful conversations with her 16-year-old son, but he was completely uninterested. The last thing he wanted to do was spend time talking with her.

But he did love movies. So she began scanning movie trailers, seeking out the films that might be most interesting for her to see with her son—and hopefully talk about afterward. When those movies hit the theaters, she would offer to take her son. He almost always accepted, and they would usually have pretty good conversations on the drive home.

Plus, just because kids say they don't want to talk to their parents, we can't assume they really mean it. I'll never forget hearing the story of Jin, a pretty rough 17-year-old whose single dad sent her to a Christian school in hopes that it would "straighten her out." Whether it was because her friends were going or because Jin warmed up to "the whole God thing," Jin signed up for the school's spring break mission trip to Guatemala.

On the flight down, Jin ended up sitting next to Joe, the school's campus pastor. For the first few hours, Jin was her normal tough self. She put on her earphones and mostly ignored Joe. He tried to ask her questions about her family, but Jin summarized her relationship with her dad by saying, "I asked him to leave me alone. And he does."

Throughout the mission trip, the Lord worked in Jin and she softened. By the end of the trip, she confessed to Joe through her tears, "I wish my dad hadn't done what I asked. I wish he hadn't left me alone."

Jin, so do I.

Leverage Point 3: Help Parents Develop Their Own Sticky Faith Rituals

"We as parents can't rely on the church," Kymira told me. "We have to be involved."

Kymira's determination to be involved in her junior high son's life was music to my ears. To put feet to her conviction, she and her husband, Kyle's stepdad, have developed a weekly discipleship time with 14-year-old Kyle. Using a small group curriculum recommended by Kyle's youth pastor, Kymira and her husband take turns going out for dessert with Kyle on Thursday evenings, and they use the curriculum as a springboard to talk with Kyle about both Scripture and what's going on in his life. During these weekly parent-son discussions, introverted Kyle has opened up about bullying at school and other peer pressures he never would have shared during this busy family's typical schedule. According to Kymira, part of the power of this Sticky Faith ritual is that Kyle "has our full and complete attention for an hour. . . . He has space to have a relationship with us as a teenager instead of as a child."

Maybe an idea like that won't connect with families in your

ministry, either because of who they are or because of who their kids are. Or maybe it will work well for a time but then begin to feel stale. Your goal is to help families find what works best for them, which often means they will need to be creative, organic, and spontaneous.

In addition to helping parents develop rituals that they can experience together with their kids, you can also encourage parents to develop rituals that help their kids connect with other adults in meaningful ways. One example of doing this comes from Reggie Joiner and the team at reThink Ministries, whose "orange" philosophy (in which the "yellow" of the light of Christ in the church and the "red" of the heart in the family unite for a greater, more synergistic "orange" impact on kids and adults) parallels our approach to building Sticky Faith. In *Parenting Beyond Your Capacity*, Reggie's coauthor, Carey Nieuwhof, shares about a powerful 5:1 intergenerational ritual he developed for his own son, Jordan, as he was entering adolescence.

When Jordan turned 13, Carey sat down with him and together they chose five men whom they both admired. Carey approached the men individually, asking each if he would spend one day with Jordan that summer. They could do whatever they wanted to do for that day, but Carey hoped they would share one spiritual truth and one life truth (i.e., good advice) during the course of their conversations.

A few of the men took Jordan camping; another took him to work. One of the five was a police chaplain who took Jordan for a ride in a police cruiser. At the end of the summer, the five men gathered with Jordan and Carey for a barbecue, and Jordan shared from a journal what had most impacted him during each of those five special days. Jordan presented each of the five men with a Bible with the man's name inscribed on the cover. Each man took a few minutes to comment on his time with Jordan and the ways he saw God at work in Jordan's life. Afterward, they all gathered around Jordan and laid hands on him in prayer. Many of the men shared, "I wish someone had done that for me when I was 13."[7]

When Carey's second son, Sam, completed the same mentoring

process when he turned 13, one highlight was the five mentors sharing how their times with Sam had impacted them. In fact, that final barbecue dinner was so powerful that the five men asked if they could gather together every year, if that was okay with Sam. Sam agreed, and they are already planning next year's dinner.

You can also encourage parents to develop rituals that are less time- and energy-intensive, such as:

Dinners with Special Adults. One friend of mine has asked her daughters to name five adults they respect and want to be like. Now my friend knows who to invite for dinner when her girls have a free evening.

Workplace Visits with Mentors. Another family I know developed a ritual that involved asking a few male friends if each would allow the family's two 13-year-old sons to accompany him to work one day. The boys spent two hours with each man at his workplace, shadowing him as he did his job. At some point during those two hours, the boys were given a few minutes to ask each man questions such as: What's the hardest part about being a man? What's the hardest part about following God? Looking back over your life, what do you wish you had done differently? Their sons still stay in touch with these men, and these experiences also encouraged the boys to seek out other male mentors as they have moved through high school and are now in college.

Special Experiences Rather Than Presents. One mom I met during our research asked friends or relatives who might normally give her kids a birthday gift to give them experiences instead. Instead of giving her kids a gift certificate or a new sweater, these folks took them to a movie or out to dinner, thereby building a stickier relationship.

Special Advice or Encouragement. Parents can invite adults who are close to their child to gather together, perhaps at a birthday or holiday celebration, and share either advice or words of encouragement with their child. If these adults can write down their counsel and present it in a book or folder, then the youth will have a permanent reminder of his or her support team.

Thanking Adults. One family at our church flipped this idea and had their kids invite adults who had been special to them to their high school graduation parties. The kids then went around the room, thanking each adult and sharing how each had personally impacted them.

Faith Ceremonies. One family who lives about an hour from Fuller decided to host their son's baptism at their home, instead of their church facility. They invited family members, as well as church members who had invested in their son, to attend and bring their eighth grader a simple gift with spiritual symbolism, such as a small painting or sculpture, or something from nature. Through this gathering of family and close friends in the family home, these parents created a ritual that, like a Jewish *bar mitzvah,* provided a powerful communal celebration of their son's spiritual milestone.

Tough Questions Related to Sticky Families

What do I do when I don't want the kids in my ministry to have the faith of their parents? For some youth leaders, the reality of parents' enormous influence on kids isn't inspiring; it's depressing. As we look at the anemic faith of the parents of the kids we work with, we may shudder to think our youth group kids might end up with the same shriveled faith.

If you are concerned about the faith of your kids' parents, a wise first step is often to talk with the pastor or leader who most closely relates with your kids' parents—whether that's an adult ministry pastor, a Sunday school teacher, or even your senior pastor. Share your observations and see how they compare with what they've experienced. Together you may be able to pinpoint certain weak areas and devise some sort of plan that might help strengthen those muscles.

Having said that, we youth leaders would be wise to heed the advice of leadership theorist Max De Pree: "The first responsibility of a leader is to define reality."[8] So let's define the reality of your role as a youth leader in parents' faith development: It's mostly out of your control. If you are concerned about the shrinking faith of parents, focus on what you can control: the other adults you invite to spend time with kids in your ministry.

Plus, the good news is that every one of us, including the very parents we are talking about, is on a spiritual journey. None of us has arrived yet, but each step along the way has value and significance. Even parents whose faith seems rather anemic may have worthwhile experiences with Jesus that they can share with their kids. There might be much more happening spiritually with parents than we know.

What's my role with parents who don't yet know the Lord? When it comes to parents who have not developed a personal relationship with Christ, the good news is that your kids can be a catalyst for their parents' faith. While you don't want to pressure them or make them feel like it's up to them to "convert" their parents, you can help your kids be involved in their parents' journey by asking questions like: What's God doing with your mom? What signs of openness are you seeing in your dad? I had coffee with another youth leader recently who told me that it was only after she became a Christian in eighth grade that her mom made the decision to follow Christ. We never know whom the Lord will use to draw people to himself.

In the meantime, kids who don't come from Christian families should be at the top of your list of kids who need 5:1 relationships. Other caring adults can help provide the spiritual scaffolding those kids need to grow.

Why should I try to partner with parents when all they do is criticize me? If you haven't been criticized by a parent, then you haven't been in youth ministry for very long. When a parent (or anyone else, for that matter) points out something they wish were different about you or your ministry, listen carefully. Ninety percent of the time there is at least a kernel of truth behind that criticism, and that is what you can listen for. If you don't quite have ears to hear that truth yourself, vet what you've been told with a few other trusted parents to get their opinions.

For more on how to handle conflict, visit www.stickyfaith.org.

How do I help parents whose kids have already shelved their faith? Every time I speak to parents, at least one of them approaches me afterward with teary eyes, grieving over a child who has drifted from the Lord. As a leader, what do you do when that happens?

When kids put their faith in an identity lockbox (see chapter 3), it's so tempting for parents to think that if they just manipulate a few details of the situation, their child will remove his or her faith from that lockbox and close the box permanently. Parents often think, "If my daughter will just come to church with me at Christmas when she's home from college, she'll realize how much she needs Jesus," or "If I just invite that nice young lady from church over for dinner, my son will want to go back to church again." Of course, God can use a dinner or a church service to draw kids back to him. But as we've talked with kids and families nationwide, that's not how it usually happens.

It's usually through relationship. Please tell parents that far more important than twisting kids' arms to get them to darken the door at church is to make sure they know that whatever doors they may crash through in their personal and spiritual lives, their parents love them and are there for them—no matter what. The same unconditional love of God that sticks with us is what we want parents—and ourselves, for that matter—to lavish on students.

For more on how to help parents in this situation, see the final chapter of the *Sticky Faith* parenting book coauthored by Kara Powell and Chap Clark.

sticky discussion questions

1. Do you agree with the idea that, in general, "When it comes to kids' faith, parents get what they are"? As you think about a few specific kids in your ministry, do you end up agreeing with the quote more or less?

2. What prevents the parents you know from talking about faith and life with their kids?

3. Which story (or stories) in this chapter would be the most motivating or encouraging to the parents in your ministry?

4. On a scale of 1 to 10 (10 being "strongly agree"), how strongly do you agree with the advice that parents should never explain something to their kids if they can ask a question instead? Is this principle also true in your own relationships with youth group kids?

5. What ideas do you have for training that could help parents be catalysts in developing their kids' Sticky Faith?

7

sticky youth groups

My high school youth group experience was the best time of my life. I could not even begin to explain. I think that it most significantly affected my self-confidence. It allowed me to become who I truly am—and if it were not for my youth group friends, I do not know what I would do.
—Daria

I think my experience was pretty beneficial at first. Then my youth pastor quit, and the person after her quit, and the person we finally ended up with I didn't know. I never really felt close to my youth group, I never really fit in. It felt like there was a lack of leadership because too many classes of kids had seen youth directors come and go, and there didn't seem to be any great need to get close to anyone anymore. I guess the feeling which settled in, at least for me, was apathy.
—Kenny

If anything, my youth group experience prepared me well in that I had low expectations for a community of Christians.
—James

"My youth pastor was one of my best friends." This encouraging quote from a *New York Times* article by George Fox student Dustin Junkert echoes the stories of students we've all known.[1] Students like Dustin sail through our ministries like all-stars, then graduate with high youth group honors if they didn't have sex or drink alcohol.

But before we're too quick to congratulate Dustin's youth pastor (or ourselves), we need to pay close attention to the very *first* line of Dustin's essay: "I grew up quietly and without thought."

Ouch.

Because Dustin was such a great kid, little attention was given to his questions and struggles about faith. Students like Dustin often leave our ministries and experience a dramatic deconstruction of faith during their freshman year. That's exactly what happened to Dustin as he came face-to-face with all kinds of questions he'd never before considered (and this was at a small Christian college).

The good news is that after Dustin spent a year thinking his faith had ended, in a moment it all became clear again. Dustin realized, "All I'd been waiting for was to know that to admit doubt was not to lose faith." It was the beginning of a whole new conversation with God.

Our hunch is that the Dustins in our ministries would love to begin those kinds of conversations *before* college, rather than grow up "quietly and without thought." Inconveniently, that may require re-envisioning youth ministry as usual.

It's generally agreed in the youth ministry world that youth group relationships and environment matter. But beyond that general agreement, have we really grasped the most significant ways they matter? Is it possible that some of what we think makes a good youth ministry environment is actually sabotaging students' faith?

The Sticky Faith findings we share in this chapter have stretched us to think harder about what really counts in youth ministry—for Dustin and thousands of others like him.

Sticky Findings

Students show up at your youth group because they like you. Seriously.

This is good news. In fact, get ready to pat yourself on the back. Nearly 80 percent of high school seniors in our study cited "I like my youth pastor" as the top reason for their being part of the youth ministry. And when looking *back* to high school from college, students single out leaders as what was most significant about youth group.

Certainly, we all want to be liked by the youth connected to our ministries. It's flattering to know that our students really like us and that we're a primary reason many of them are part of the group. But if we're the main reason kids are attending, it does raise an important question: Are our ministries centered on Jesus . . . or on us?

In some situations this false, leader-centered ministry is blatantly obvious. A charismatic leader builds a following around his or her personality, quickly growing numbers and enthusiasm, and often stirring deep emotional response. Then there's the fallout—when the leader moves on, for whatever reason, it's dramatic. Early in my ministry, I (Brad) lived through the fallout after a key leader's departure left the other leaders, kids, and parents questioning not only the youth group and the church, but also their faith. In fact, I almost bailed on youth ministry myself. As it turns out, "I like my youth pastor" isn't the best adhesive we could use to inspire Sticky Faith.

At least part of kids' motivation to come to youth group is because they want to connect with God.

There's hope! You're probably wondering what else was on the motivation list for being part of a youth group. So here's the rest of the top five:

2. I learn about God there.
3. I feel comfortable there.
4. I can really worship God there.
5. I've always gone.

Thankfully, the presence of an attractive, charismatic youth leader isn't the *only* reason students are involved in a youth ministry. This top-five list is certainly a mixed bag (items 3 and 5 hint at complacency), but we can be encouraged that students come—at least in part—to learn about and worship God.

✳ Looking back on their youth group, only one in five students felt "My youth leaders really knew me."

Despite being drawn to us, many students feel something disturbingly different in return: unknown. One student shared, "I wish that a leader had paid more attention to me. I wasn't one of the kids that had obvious struggles and wasn't really outgoing, so I often felt overlooked. I didn't always go to things because I didn't think it mattered or anyone would even notice that I wasn't there."

On the other hand, the effects of feeling known by adults during high school stretched across several years afterward. The more college students and other youth group graduates continued to feel support from their high school youth pastor or other adults from their home church, the stickier their faith was three years later.[2]

✳ One of the most important things adult leaders can do is to help students apply faith to their daily lives.

Among the 13 different ways adults support high school kids, two variables stood out as significantly related to Sticky Faith over time: feeling sought out by adults and feeling like those adults "helped me to realistically apply my faith to my daily life."[3] Especially as we wrestle with how to train our staff and adult volunteers, helping kids connect the dots between their faith and their everyday lives should take priority if we're looking for long-term impact.

✳ Kids don't feel as close to their youth group friends as we might think.

Friendships within our ministries aren't as strong as we might expect. Peers in youth group are neither a big reason for attending (ranked sixteenth on a list of motivations), nor seen as a key source of support (ranked fourth out of five options, behind friends outside of youth group).

While we youth leaders do *a lot* of talking (and writing, and teaching) about "building community" in our youth groups, our rhetoric may not be translating into reality. But the news about relationships within our youth ministries isn't all gloomy . . .

✸ Looking back a year later, the three things students remember as most significant about youth group are:

1. The adults involved
2. The community formed
3. Friendships

While our students may not be as closely connected to one another as we might hope, many students *do* carry warm memories of the relationships developed in their youth ministries. College seems to bring a new appreciation. Given the radical changes in the social and spiritual landscape beyond youth group, adult investment and peer friendships from youth ministry days stand out as bright spots.

✸ What did students want to see more of in their high school youth ministries? Time for deep conversation.

In chapter 5, we shared about students' desire for deeper ways to serve (items 2 and 3 below). Let's look at the full list of what students wanted more of from their youth groups:

> If drawing directly from my high school youth ministry, I would define Christianity as being about pizza parties and entertainment alternatives.
>
> —Rodney

1. Time for deep conversation
2. Mission trips
3. Service projects
4. Accountability
5. One-on-one time with leaders

Note that kids weren't asking for more games. In fact, games were at the bottom of this list. Alex showed up in our youth ministry with one plea: "Please don't make me play games!" A good-natured sophomore who had suffered through years of game-centric youth groups, he was desperately looking for something deeper. Kids are hungering for less time in mixers, competitions, and (if we're honest) time-wasters, and more time invested in the things that require little money or planning: conversations. Especially conversations where an adult leader gives careful, personal attention to listening to a student.

Retreat experiences are key in helping kids develop Sticky Faith.

Most of us youth leaders count on retreat experiences to bolster kids' faith. Turns out those hopes are well-founded. One of the specific youth group activities we tracked was participation in retreats. And our studies found that retreat experiences (overnight, away from home) were important to faith growth for the students in our study. In fact, when analyzed across all three years of the survey, attending retreats during high school was one of the few youth group activities independently correlated with Sticky Faith.

Student leaders tend to stick with faith.

While you might not have guessed that worshiping with the congregation would be such an important Sticky Faith factor (see chapter 4), you probably would have assumed that involving kids in leadership would be. We have good news on this front. Those students who participated in leadership in their youth ministry and/or led middle school or elementary kids showed stronger faith three years later than those who didn't.

During both high school and college, students devote very little time or attention to central spiritual disciplines like prayer and Bible study.

We youth workers invest a lot of time and energy (not to mention anxiety) providing engaging themes, inspiring messages, and decent worship bands for our ministries. Yet the majority of students exit with very little grounding in some of the core practices of faith.

At the end of high school, prayer was the discipline students reported practicing most commonly. But we'd be lying if we said we were encouraged by the frequency. Less than half of the surveyed students said they prayed daily, and only 83 percent claimed to pray at least once a week.

Bible reading showed up even less frequently: 42 percent said they read the Bible weekly, and only 12 percent read their Bibles daily. The bottom line: Only about half of the high school seniors graduating from our youth groups pick up a Bible once a week or toss up a prayer once a day. These percentages remain fairly stable across the transition to college.[4]

> Your faith is not spoon-fed to you anymore after high school. You don't have anyone looking over you when you step into college to make sure you are going to church or to see if you are getting plugged in somewhere or to see if you're having a "quiet time." You now have to claim it on your own and be able to walk on your own two feet.
>
> —Julie

Most kids doubt their faith in high school, but few talk about those doubts. Yet the students who feel most free to express doubts and discuss personal problems with youth leaders and their youth groups show more Sticky Faith.

Many of us come from traditions or training that suggests that doubt is troubling or even sinful. But our research shows there's a lot to be said for doubt forming our faith in stronger and perhaps more lasting ways. And an environment that gives students freedom to express doubts and struggles actually promotes Sticky Faith.

Seventy percent of the students in our study reported that they had doubts in high school about what they believed about God and the Christian faith, and just as many felt like they wanted to talk with their youth leaders about their doubts. Yet less than half of those students actually talked with youth leaders about them. Likewise, less than half talked with their youth group peers about their doubts. Among those who did talk with leaders or peers, about half found these conversations helped them.

So if you do the math here (and we can't resist), that means that seven of every ten students is struggling with doubts—but only one or two of those ten is likely to have had helpful conversations about those doubts with youth leaders or friends during high school. That means a lot of kids are wrestling with their doubts alone and in silence. One girl put it this way:

> *I wish I'd felt more able to confide honestly in someone. I loved my mentor all through high school group, but I felt like if I told her the whole truth about my life, she would look at me completely differently because of the things she had said in the past regarding situations I was struggling with.*

When we asked our students in college to reflect back on the doubts they remembered having during high school, here are some of the things they recall doubting (listed in no particular order):

- "If God would still love me if I had sex. Most of my doubts circulated around sex, actually."
- "I would doubt if I was worth anything."
- "If God really existed."
- "If God was real and if he would forgive me for all the bad things I had done and was doing."
- "Why God would allow terrible things to happen if he was so loving and sensitive."
- "All across the board."
- "Why do I feel like I am never able to hear God?"
- "Homosexuality (Is it really such a bad thing?)"
- "Do non-Christians really go to hell, even if they are good people?"

Overall, the doubts tended to cluster around four central questions:

1. Does God exist?
2. Does God love me?
3. Am I living the life God wants?
4. Is Christianity true/the only way to God?

Creating a youth ministry where students can talk about these questions honestly, openly, and without fear could be one of the best things we do to help build Sticky Faith.

Sticky Faith Made Practical

Try as we might, none of us can produce the "perfect" youth ministry environment. This chapter certainly won't give you all the answers to creating the stickiest youth group around. But hopefully the following Sticky Faith tools can be useful to assess where you are and where you'd like to be.

Specifically, let's look at the implications of our Sticky Findings in terms of constructing a Sticky Youth Group environment, fostering Sticky Relationships, and reimagining Sticky Programs.

Constructing a Sticky Youth Group Environment

Declare and defend a safe zone where doubts and struggles can be shared without fear.

If students who feel safe to express their doubts in their high school youth groups seem to actually have a *stronger* faith as seniors and then in college, why do many of us teach and preach faith as the absence of doubt? Some level of doubt is normative to the Christian life, yet we often pretend "Good Christians" are immune to it. This perception can be intensified by the letdowns that can follow retreat and camp highs and hype, haunting students who wake up the next week and don't "feel God" as viscerally as before. Somehow, we've failed to embrace the teaching of Jude 22 to "be merciful to those who doubt."

Students need leaders whose faith is marked by a humility that recognizes that God is big enough for kids' questions—and bigger than our answers. This may mean lowering our performance expectations of superstar students like Dustin. These kids often feel the least able to share their struggles, for fear of letting the youth pastor down or being seen as "less spiritual" than others think.

> I have had more life experiences over the last four years since high school, and I've just been in more difficult situations and been faced with more challenges. I think that has definitely solidified my faith more. I've had to ask more difficult questions, which at first makes my faith rocky; but then once I work through those questions, that makes it more solid. So my faith has definitely grown stronger today than it was years ago or even weeks ago.
>
> —Alan

We need to remember that nearly every kid we work with will doubt his or her faith at some point—whether that struggle is obvious or not. Our responsibility to them includes creating safe places for questions that emerge along the way. In small group settings, mentoring relationships, and in the context of the broader youth ministry, how are doubts and struggles being voiced, and how are they being received?

In an interview with Derek Melleby from the Center for Parent/Youth Understanding, sociologist Tim Clydesdale relayed the following findings from his research on college students, specifically those who had walked away from faith:

In many cases, these teens reported having important questions regarding faith during early adolescence (12-14 years old) that were ignored by their parents or pastors rather than taken seriously and engaged thoughtfully. It is in early adolescence that faith trajectories (along with other life trajectories) are set. . . . Sadly, most youth ministries are long on fun and fluff and short on listening and thoughtful engagement. The former produces a million paper boats; the latter produces a handful of seaworthy ships. Launching a million paper boats is an amazing spectacle on a clear summer day, but only a ship can weather storms and cross oceans.[5]

Paper boats versus seaworthy ships. Which are we building?

Here are a few practical ideas from other youth workers who are committed to creating open spaces in their ministries where doubts and struggles can be shared:

Bible Fight Club. Open the floor periodically for kids to ask hard questions about the Bible without any repercussions, even if leaders don't have good answers at the time.

Honesty Box. Create a place where anonymous questions about God, the Bible, or living as a Christian can be submitted at any time. Periodically, leaders can address one or more of the questions from the front.

Role-Playing. In your adult ministry team, practice responding to situations where kids raise hard questions. Use role-play as a teaching tool for adult leaders to learn to be more accepting of doubt as part of the faith-development process.

Talk about Crises. When troubling local or global events raise tough questions about God's goodness and power, make space for conversations about what kids are thinking and feeling.

Teach about Doubt. Take opportunities to teach on doubt, particularly when you encounter expressions of doubt or uncertainty in Scripture.

Practice Lament. One of the gifts of Scripture is its insistence on the practice of lament. For example, more than one-third of the psalms are considered laments in which the author cries out to God in pain, suffering, and doubt. Some laments are personal, others are corporate—but they serve to remind us that it's okay to express our struggles and ask God hard questions. By weaving them into our corporate worship and prayer life, we open up the possibility that kids might feel freer to share their own hard questions, and maybe even write their own psalms of lament.

One church in our Sticky Faith Learning Cohort is working hard to create space for doubt in the midst of its confirmation program. At the conclusion of the six-month process, most students write a statement of faith. One student, however, felt safe enough to write a "Statement of Doubt" instead. This allowed her to share openly with the community that her own journey of faith wasn't yet at the point of trusting Christ. Several months later, she came to the point where she had wrestled through her doubts and decided to be baptized as an expression of her newfound trust. Alongside her were several adults who had supported her, prayed for her, and walked with her through her valley of doubt to the other side of faith.

> For more resources on practicing lament in youth ministry, see www.stickyfaith.org.

Checking In. Take the common youth group practice of checking in with one another and turn it into an opportunity to listen more closely. One group we know asks each person, "How are you doing, really?" After each individual shares, the rule is that no one is allowed to respond. This time is not about fixing problems or offering advice, but just about listening well.

56 Seconds. One ministry shared that they close each session of their fifth-and-sixth-grade group with 56 seconds of silence, during which kids can write down any question on a note card. The hope is to make asking questions a normal part of faith development, even if all those questions don't get answered.

Center our ministries in prayer and Scripture.

I (Brad) recently received a Facebook message from a student who is now a year out of college. Ross was from an unchurched family and had come into our group during his junior year of high school. The faith transformation he experienced over his last two years of high school—including his baptism—inspired us all. But I'd lost touch with him after his first semester of college.

Curious to hear from him several years later, I asked how things were going in his relationship with God. I got a lengthy response. Ross spent the better part of college "running from God" (his words), but eventually God "caught up" with him.

His recent spiritual journey has included learning how to pray. Ross reflected that he never really learned how to pray or relate to God in high school. While it wasn't meant as a criticism of me or our ministry, I couldn't help but wonder: What could we have done differently to prepare Ross?

Too often we relegate prayer to the position of an add-on "if we have time" or a token way we start or end our programming. But how can we reimagine the place of prayer in our programs and relationships in ways that will inspire kids to pursue the God who is pursuing them? The same question applies for Scripture.

In his work with the Youth Ministry and Spirituality Project, Mark Yaconelli has encouraged many youth leaders to make contemplative practices a centerpiece of their ministries, not just occasional extras for times when they feel like lighting candles or creating elaborate prayer stations. Often these regular practices include prayers like the Ignatian *examen* (or prayer of review) and Scripture reflection in the style of *lectio divina* ("divine reading"), where time and space are created for meditation on the text rather than teaching from it. [6]

> My youth pastor would always emphasize that it's not just about saying you're a Christian; it's about acting out your faith through living out Jesus' love. From the beginning, I was taught the importance of reading Scripture and praying, and so that built habits that have benefited me enormously in college.
> —Evie

Centering our ministries in prayer and Scripture cannot happen unless we center our own lives in prayer and Scripture. The FYI web site (www.fulleryouthinstitute.org) contains dozens of resources on topics such as rest, Sabbath, and self-care that offer ideas for prayers and contemplative practices you could try, including two self-led retreat guides.

Train volunteers and staff in good listening and basic counseling skills.

Recently a high school pastor relayed the conversation he'd had with his small group of ninth grade boys during a series on "Love,

> I really appreciated that it wasn't just during the allotted small group time that I was invested in; it was beyond the allotted time that these staff people were taking time to meet with me and invest in me.
>
> —Bella

Sex, and Dating." In an effort to help students think about how they are God's masterpieces, he asked the guys what they had that was most valuable. The first kid who answered said, "I know what you want me to say: It's my virginity, right?" So that was the answer he gave.

The rest of the group followed by sharing about what was most valuable to them, with answers ranging from cameras to computers to collectibles. After hearing a few of his friends' answers, the first boy said, "Wait, so I don't have to say it's my virginity?"

How many of our kids respond to our questions by giving us pat answers, the answers they think we want to hear? When we fail to really listen to what they are saying—or aren't saying—we encourage them to fall back on pat answers. Training ourselves and our ministry volunteers in good listening skills may be as important as learning how to study and teach the Bible.

Offer a balance of support and challenge.

Along with listening well, other research points to the importance of giving both support and challenge in creating Sticky Environments for growth. Harvard developmental psychologist Robert Kegan sums this up well:

> *People grow best when they continuously experience an ingenious blend of support and challenge; the rest is commentary. Environments that are weighted too heavily in the direction of challenge without adequate support are toxic; they promote defensiveness and constriction. Those weighted too heavily toward support without adequate challenge are ultimately boring; they promote devitalization . . . [T]he balance of support and challenge leads to vital engagement.*[7]

As we seek to build Sticky Faith in kids who are already seeking to follow Christ, what can we do to foster new faith in kids who don't yet know Jesus? In one study on youth conversion, Drs. Dave Rahn and Tom Bergler found the following factors were most influential in a decision to follow Christ:

1. The nonverbal witness of their friends
2. The verbal influence of their friends
3. Their parents

In other words, unchurched kids seem most likely to respond to their own friends who both talk about and live out their faith in front of them. All of these factors were more important than youth workers' nonverbal or verbal witness.[8]

Fostering Sticky Relationships

Can I Trust You?

A few weeks ago I (Brad) was speaking to a group of new high school grads. Just before the first session, I met some of the students. Ty came up and introduced himself, then he asked what I thought was a good name for a boy "because my girlfriend's pregnant, and we're having a boy."

Gulp.

It was kind of a funny question, but he looked serious. I've known enough pregnant youth group kids that I'm not too shocked by that reality. But it's not often that a student makes that part of his *introduction.*

I think in response I said something like, "Wow, you have more than a few transitions coming up then, huh?" Ty soberly nodded his head, then his friend butted in and introduced himself.

During my talk—which focused on making the transition to college—I tried to be more sensitive to those making other kinds of transitions, like to work or family responsibilities. I kept thinking about this guy who was about to launch into fatherhood, and I wondered how it felt to be in the room with his college-bound friends launching into totally different freedoms.

After my talk, Ty came up to me again, so I took the opportunity to ask more questions. I asked him when the baby was due. He smiled and said, "Oh, I was lying about that. I just wanted to see if you were a jerk. You're not. Thanks for taking me seriously."

At first I was a little ticked off that he'd lied and that I'd been so naive. But then I realized that essentially Ty was asking, "Can I trust you?" His question was a test—or maybe a defense mechanism set up to block out adults who aren't worth listening to. The joke was on me, but I'd passed his first test and he let me see a small part of his "real" world. And part of Ty's reality is having a dad who's a bit of a jerk. Of course he'd be suspicious of someone like me.

In nearly every interaction we have with teenagers, we face some version of the "Can I trust you?" test. Sometimes it's more obvious than others. Sometimes we never know it's a test. What's important is that we take it—and them—seriously. For kids who are dying to be heard, the test offers a chance to speak trust and gain an opportunity to listen. What an honor. Here are a few suggestions for building youth ministry relationships where kids begin to trust us and let us into their worlds:[9]

Become (and stay) Jesus-centered rather than leader-centered.

In one of our Sticky Faith Summits at Fuller, we gathered incredibly sharp leaders to dialogue about preliminary findings from our study. Dr. Dave Rahn, vice president and chief ministry officer of Youth for Christ/USA, noted that there's a certain "seductiveness of fondness" that comes with ministry. By this he means it's tempting, for those of us who work with youth, to love being loved and to latch on to this feeling of affinity as a way to boost our own self-images or to keep us motivated to continue in ministry. In fact, the "Do they like me?" factor is such a strong motivating factor for many folks that they bow out of ministry when they feel like affirmation has waned.

In contrast to those who seek glory and affirmation for themselves, consider the example of John the Baptist. This man lived and died pointing to Jesus. In one of the few quotes of his preserved in Scripture, he says, "He must become greater; I must become less" (John 3:30). When the emphasis in ministry is on bringing glory to God, not the youth leader, kids can begin to create dependence on the One to whom we point.

Think more creatively about ministry volunteer recruiting.

Long-term relationships with adults matter in the lives of the kids we work with. These relationships matter when kids are in high school and as they cross the transition into young adulthood. While most of us already know this intuitively, we sometimes recruit volunteers as if we've never heard it. Many churches have a typical (but unwritten) profile for youth ministry volunteers, and it tends to go something like: "Young college-age hip kid with availability for the next year or so." These folks shouldn't be excluded from youth ministry (Kara, Cheryl, and I all started youth ministry as college students ourselves). But when we think this is the only acceptable profile for youth ministry volunteers, we set up our students to think the same way. This practice tends to lead students to over-attachment and frequent disappointment as younger leaders often move on. And it deprives teens of the opportunity to build long-lasting relationships with adults.

How could we expand our volunteer profiles to include adults of many different ages and life stages? Empty-nesters and senior adults sometimes have more time available than college students do, as well as having a wealth of invaluable life experience to share with kids. What's more, these folks are much more likely to still be around and part of the church a year, three years, and ten years down the line when our students need ongoing stability from their faith family. As we discussed in chapter 4, the more intergenerational relationships, the better.

The importance of longevity extends to the youth pastor, too. One of the themes that stood out from our interviews was the pain students felt when a youth pastor moved on. In particular, kids who experienced multiple youth pastor transitions during their high

When I didn't feel comfortable wrestling through issues with my parents, my small group leader was there for me. For six years, (unreal, right?) she was committed to hosting us silly girls in her living room, taking us out for coffee, and being real with us as we awkwardly struggled through high school. The youth ministry was where faith really became my own.

—Chloe

school years often became disillusioned and disconnected from the youth ministry.

Rethink the ways we "build community" in youth ministry.

Let's be honest. We speak a great line about developing community in our ministries, but too often that means something like playing competitive dodgeball for half of our Wednesday night youth group meeting and then going out for ice cream afterward. Neither of those activities is *necessarily* bad, but they don't equate with community.

Besides games and food, how else do we bring kids together (often kids from multiple schools and neighborhoods) and get them to not only like each other, but also form lasting spiritual bonds? Below are a few ideas we've gathered from others that you and your ministry might consider.

Create stability.

Many students experience chaos as the norm of their day-to-day lives. They are shuttled from swim team to voice lessons to tutoring, and many are juggled back and forth between divorced parents. Not to mention the disorientation a typical high school day holds.

In contrast, we can cast a vision for a youth ministry that serves as one consistent, stable, "normal" part of their otherwise chaotic weeks. Creating ministries that say, "We're here today, we'll be here next week and the week after that, and we'll continue to care for you," can offer invaluable assurance to students even if it doesn't seem fresh and exciting to us. Designing small groups, mentoring relationships, or service opportunities that extend across several years can have a similar impact.

We are family.

A step further than stability, the church has the mandate to be the family of God. While that needs to be an intergenerational expression of family in order to be healthy, the youth ministry can strengthen these bonds by communicating that students are significant family members. Eating together, playing together, celebrating together, and doing whatever you do in the context of familial language contributes to the family health of your group.[10]

Reimagining Sticky Programs

While we all tout the importance of relationships in youth ministry, we also know that on some level or another we have to think programmatically as well. How can we shift our programming in ways that more effectively nurture Sticky Faith? Here are a few starters.

Get them off-site.

If carving out more time for deep conversation, creating space for sharing doubts and struggles, centering on Jesus, and building community are all Sticky Faith goals, one way youth pastors have been effectively pursuing these goals for years has been off-campus overnight retreats. While retreats can certainly be done poorly and without focus or depth, they have incredible potential to open up space and time for quality faith-building. And, at least according to our study, they can be effective in nurturing faith maturity that lasts. If you're looking for a programmatic element to ditch this year, skip the day at the amusement park before you cut the weekend retreat.

Develop competencies.

This past year I started a new adventure. I stepped away from my role as leader of one of our congregation's worship teams in order to develop a student worship team for our middle school ministry.

> In my youth group, we were pushed to be leaders and witness openly about our faith, but I felt like I received little instruction or support in how to actually do that. I felt like so much emphasis was put on DOING, but I received little instruction in why or how.
>
> —Kendra

I now have the privilege of leading this group of young singers and musicians as they work through the challenges of coming together to make music as a team and lead their peers in worship. It's messy—and it doesn't always sound good—but it's incredibly important.

One reason I'm so excited about investing in this ministry is because research points to the importance of developing competence in teenagers' lives. Not only does learning competence in an area promote overall thriving in kids, but it is also specifically tied to helping faith stick beyond high school. In both our study and others, giving students meaningful and skill-developing opportunities to serve their youth group and church matters—right now and for years to come.[11]

Give students authentic opportunities to lead—but protect them along the way.

In recent years, much of youth ministry (as well as many non-faith-based youth development efforts) has shifted toward youth "ownership" of programs and practices. When done well, this movement toward youth empowerment has great potential to build both competencies and confidence. Yet we must be careful along the way to nurture leadership without letting kids burn out or making them feel like youth group is one more place where they have to show up and perform in certain ways in order to maintain our approval.

Belinda was a gifted student leader. A youth group "superstar" from sixth grade on, Belinda had already served on our ministry's leadership team for several years by the time she reached her sophomore year. I found myself giving her responsibilities and expecting she'd complete them without being reminded or supported, then getting upset with her when she failed to follow through. It slowly became evident that rather than developing a competent young leader, I'd created an environment in which Belinda felt the same pressure to be perfect that she felt everywhere else—and ultimately I burnt out our relationship and her involvement in our ministry. What's worse, I failed to see classic signs that she was developing an eating disorder that was diminishing her body and her faith.

A student in our study expressed a similar sense of feeling overburdened with ministry responsibilities:

I was a worship leader, and my youth pastor basically handed me the position. But after giving me a ridiculous amount of responsibility, he rarely took any of it back. Also, as the leaders got to know me better, it seemed like they extended less grace to me. When I would confide in them about my life, I started to censor what I would say. As a result, it made me feel more vulnerable and less welcomed. It was hard to come to youth group feeling the same security and value from leaders as I did when I was a freshman.

On the flip side of this scenario, sometimes we ask students to make an occasional announcement or stand by the sign-in table, and we call that "leadership." What, then, does authentic and healthy ownership look like? The answer probably depends on both your context and your philosophy of leadership. But here are a few ideas from churches that have taken differing

I think that we too often expect so little from junior highers and high schoolers. We don't ask difficult questions, and we kind of dumb things down or make small challenges that seem easy for them to do. But I think it leaves them unprepared for the real questions they're going to face when they get to college. Don't be afraid to ask your kids difficult questions now and push them to ask difficult questions, and challenge them with big ideas and to build disciplined habits that will shape them in the future.

—Ian

approaches toward equipping and empowering students to serve as leaders.

One church shared that their process of cultivating leadership skills among youth begins with inviting middle school students to be part of a group whose vision is to be "A place where God is changing us so we can change the world." Half of the group's time is spent on spiritual formation practices, and the other half is on leadership development. Over time they give students responsibilities like helping with teaching elements on Sundays and planning portions of retreats.

Last year almost all of this church's student leadership group committed on their own to join the "Advent Conspiracy" (www.adventconspiracy.org), a grassroots effort to reverse consumerism at Christmas. These kids told family and friends that rather than receiving Christmas gifts, they wanted to channel the money to their church's partner ministry in Africa. So instead of opening up new clothes or gadgets for Christmas, this small group of middle school students alone contributed more than $2,500 toward orphan care. In doing so, they led the way by their example for other students to make sacrificial choices on behalf of others.

Several other churches focus on pairing high school students with adult volunteers to co-lead small groups for middle school or upper elementary ministry. This works best when students are partnered with mature adult leaders who mentor and care for their co-leaders along the way. And often these leadership pairings are more organic than programmed, based either on students' initiative or invitation of the small group leader. As April Diaz from Newsong church in Irvine, California, commented, "One of the reasons it's worked well is because of the intergenerational relationships themselves. Students have been able to connect with older moms who are leading small groups, college students, and other adults. They are like sponges in these relationships."

The message we have heard most from youth workers was well described by Josh Bishop of Mars Hill Bible Church in Grand Rapids,

Real Leadership

I've too often seen the term *leadership* partnered with *program*. But the idea of creating some kind of team or experience that some students have access to and others don't is troubling to me. The high school ministry I inherited had a few student leaders whose main role was to welcome other students from the stage and make announcements. Shortly after I started, a sophomore student emailed me and asked: "Who are you going to find to do announcements this year? Jim and Sarah are really cool, but they both graduated. You need to find someone else cool to do it. I would like to help out on Wednesday nights, but I'm not cool enough to be on stage." I realized that student "leadership" was a token position that communicated "coolness" and "superiority" to other students. Instead of encouraging other students to help lead, we had created a division between the "cool" and the "uncool."

Our programs, retreats, mission trips, and service projects should be environments where we intentionally and subversively invite students to discover learning and leadership on their own initiative and at their own pace. For example, our high school ministry participated in our annual spring break trip to Mississippi doing Katrina relief work. There's only so much planning that can take place in advance—much of the trip must be figured out while we're on the ground. This creates opportunities for students to step up and make the most of the experience while leading others—or to step back and become frustrated when plans change or expectations aren't met. At the end of the trip, one high school sophomore said, "I was scared to come on this trip. I don't like being away from home, and I don't like manual labor. This trip has helped me to realize that I actually love the things I used to be afraid of." This student was a leader in every sense of the word during this trip—but she never would have signed up to be a leader or been nominated to be a leader.

—Matt Laidlaw, Mars Hill Bible Church

a member of our Sticky Faith Learning Cohort: "Students who want to be involved should see themselves as servants more than as leaders. Servanthood is a central part of the kind of faith we hope sticks." In other words, student leadership isn't grounded in competition or superiority, but in being willing to serve humbly—and perhaps not even be identified as a "leader."

Program less.

As we've discussed what students want and need from our youth ministry programs, the question we often land on goes something like this: How do we create more space and time for the deep conversations kids are hungering for, both with leaders and one another? In other words, how do we program *less*? What do we need to give up in order to gain that depth we hope for? These are questions we should continually consider whenever we meet with our teams to plan out program and events calendars.

A youth worker shared with me recently that the past summer had been "delightful." When I asked why, she said they'd eliminated summer meetings altogether; and since they didn't have the funding to take their usual mission trip, they essentially deprogrammed the entire summer. They collaborated with other local youth ministries to do once-weekly programming, like gathering in a local park or at each other's churches. But otherwise the summer was wide open. This led to more space for reflection, more space for relationship building, and more space for connecting with parents and leaders to prepare for the coming school year.

You may not be able to deprogram your whole summer. But perhaps you can use this research to support your plea to back off on hyper-programmed summers (or other seasons, for that matter). Or maybe you could take two or three weeks or even a month off of regular programming for planning, preparation, and retreat. Not only could it strengthen the path to Sticky Faith for your students, but it could also lay the path to a more balanced life for you as a youth leader.

sticky discussion questions

1. How do you make space for struggles, questions, and doubts to be voiced and heard in your ministry? What could you do to foster a more open environment for sharing?

2. Chances are good that the older students in your ministry are longing for more time for deep conversation, as were the students in our study. What are you doing to create that room within your programs and relationships?

3. Draw a line down the center of a piece of paper. Label the first column "Sticky Environment" and the second "Not-so-Sticky Environment." Then do a quick analysis of your ministry's programs and relationships, jotting down practices in the appropriate column based on your assessment after reading this chapter. Then flip the paper over and brainstorm ideas for either eliminating or re-imagining the Not-so-Sticky practices in ways that contribute to a stickier youth group environment. Share your lists with your team, or do the exercise together and see what emerges.

4. Contact some former "student leaders" who've graduated from your ministry and get together or talk by phone, asking them to evaluate the way your ministry approaches leadership and develops leaders. Looking back, what was helpful? What was not-so-helpful or even harmful? What's most meaningful to them now from those experiences? How do they see things differently now that they are beyond high school? Take this feedback to your ministry team and consider how your approach to student leadership might be modified.

8

sticky seniors

There was no transition at all. It was "Hey, you're in high school,"
"Hey look, you're a senior," then BAM! it was, "See ya 'round, kid."
—Alex

Honestly, the transition has not been easy. My church offers noth-
ing for college students. I find I do not fit in anymore. I do not
belong to the youth group anymore, and it has been hard for me
because I was in that youth group for four years of my life.
—Jennie

I wish there was more of a transition. It seemed like when I
was done with high school, everything ended really fast. I
haven't heard from the youth pastor or the worship leader I
led music with or any other leader since that last night of
church before I left for college. That's really sad to me.
—Karina

In my early days of youth ministry, two events pretty much summed
up all I (Brad) did to prepare our graduating high school seniors for
their transition out of our youth group: Senior Graduation Sunday
and Senior Dinner. Graduation Sunday basically boiled down to a
quick handshake in front of the church and a token gift. Right on
its heels was our Senior Dinner, which had devolved into more of a
"roast" than a meaningful ritual. We did little to prepare students to
think about life—and faith—after leaving youth group.

One year, facing a close-knit but somewhat spiritually immature
group of twelfth-graders, I decided to kick it up a notch. Starting

in September of their senior year, I offered them something a little risky: breakfast once a week, cooked by me, at my house, at 7:00 a.m.

To my surprise, they showed up. Over and over again. All year long.

We talked about a lot of things that year. I was usually winging it from week to week, pulling in spiritual gifts inventories and Bible passages I thought might lead to meaningful discussions. We talked about everything from managing money and relationships to doing homework and laundry.

Ten years later, in the midst of our FYI research, I asked a few of these now-28-year-olds what they remembered about those breakfasts. None of them could remember any of the content we covered. Instead, they mentioned things like the winter day our stove wasn't working and I tried to grill the bacon on my back deck, with disastrous results. (If you've never tried it, don't.) One grad commented about the breakfasts: "Looking back on it now, what really meant the most is that you made the effort to do that for us. You made yourself available and took the time to keep us accountable as a class. There was time and space carved out for us on a regular basis in case we needed to vent something or needed extra support."

This group of students didn't all go on to be spiritual heroes; a few did, while others later walked away from faith. And to be honest, I never repeated that year's senior breakfast strategy (even though I got better at cooking bacon). The following years led to different methods for different groups, including spreading the responsibility for discipleship beyond me, the youth pastor. But the breakfast group set me on a journey of thinking harder about how to prepare graduating high school seniors for a lifetime of Sticky Faith.

Like the rest of this book, this chapter pulls from our research with students, but also draws heavily on our conversations with hundreds of youth workers across the country over the past several years. Whether your senior strategy thus far has boiled down to handing out Bibles in front of your congregation on a spring Sunday, or whether you've been cooking breakfast for seniors every week, we hope these practical ideas inspire you—and even more importantly, inspire your students—toward Sticky Faith.

Sticky Findings

Only one of every seven graduates leaves youth group feeling "very prepared" for what college brings their way.

According to students themselves, most youth ministries aren't setting them up for success in the transition to college. This is especially tragic because our research shows that feeling prepared really matters. The more prepared students feel—whether that be to make friends or to handle new lifestyle choices—the more likely their faith is to grow.

Seniors want our help.

When we asked youth group graduates what advice they would give youth leaders, the number one piece of advice—by far—was to better prepare graduates for what they would face after high school. Specifically, students requested structured training on the transition and how they could best get ready. Alums wished that when they had been seniors, they had heard more from college students and other grads so they could learn from their experiences and ask them questions.

Graduates from our groups want to hear from us, and our contact makes a difference in their long-term faith.

When college students were asked what they wish had been different about their high school youth groups, the most common responses centered on wishing they'd kept in contact with friends and leaders post-graduation. A quarter of the students noted specifically that they *wanted* someone from their high school youth group to contact them at college, *but no one did*. As it turns out, staying in

I think one of the main reasons I got so involved in ministry was that the first week I was on campus, I was looking for a campus ministry. My youth pastor encouraged me that I needed to find community as soon as possible, not to put it on the back burner. Don't skip church that first week because it just makes it easier to skip it the second week and then the eighth week . . .

—Young Mi

The longer you wait, the harder it is to get plugged in to a church or a campus ministry.

—Sheldon

touch with a high school youth pastor or other adult leader during the freshman year is a strong predictor of Sticky Faith.

The first two weeks of college set the trajectory for the next few years.

Over and over, students told us that the first two weeks at college are when many key decisions are made—about drinking and other high-risk behaviors, right along with choosing whether to go to church or campus ministry. Many of these decisions are influenced by the new friends freshmen surround themselves with and the new situations in which they put themselves. Most students are totally unprepared for the intensity of those first days and weeks, and have no strategy for how to make decisions during that critical time.

Most students don't know how to find a church in college.

Though nearly all youth workers hope their grads will get involved with a church in college, less than 40 percent of students felt like their youth ministry actually prepared them to find a new church. Not surprisingly, finding a church was mentioned as one of the three most difficult parts of the transition to college (the others were loneliness and finding new friends).

Engaging in a church or campus group during the freshman year makes a big difference.

For students living away from home, connecting with either an off-campus church or an on-campus Christian fellowship is positively linked with Sticky Faith in the freshman year and beyond. Involvement with on-campus fellowships shows the strongest correlation with measures of Sticky Faith during freshman year.

I didn't think I really needed to go to church to be a strong Christian. But after being away from church completely while I studied abroad, I went back to church one Sunday and saw people caring for each other in a way that I had not experienced outside of the church body.

—Amy

Unfortunately, during the fall of freshman year, only 40 percent of former youth group students said they attended an on-campus fellowship once a week or more, and 57 percent were attending church once a week or more.

Managing daily life is overwhelming for most college students, leaving no time or energy to think about faith.

During their freshman year, nearly half the students in our study felt anxious because so much was suddenly left up to them to decide.[1] We also found that students struggle most to integrate their faith with how they use time and money.

Yet both time management and money management are big hang-ups in college. Given that the average credit card debt of a college student is more than $3,000 and half of undergraduates own four or more credit cards, finances are clearly an area where students need help.[2] And the new time flexibility also creates major challenges. As one student shared with us, "In high school, *everything* was scheduled. In college, I was finished with classes by noon and had all day to do whatever I wanted. And no one asks you if you went to class or did your homework. I had to learn how to manage my own time well."

✖ Encountering other students who think and believe differently tends to strengthen faith.

Three years into college, we asked students about ways certain events challenged or strengthened their faith. The experiences most connected to Sticky Faith were interactions with other students; particularly with people of other faiths and with students of other cultures/ethnicities. We often fear that the increased diversity of life-style and belief that many students encounter in college will weaken their faith; in fact, the opposite seems to be true.

✖ Key advice from grads: Stay engaged with faith and other Christians.

When we asked former youth group graduates what they would share with a group of high school seniors about going to college, they had a lot to say. Their answers clustered into the following categories, listed in order of importance:

1. Find a faith community at college and get connected.
2. Engage with your faith, including emerging questions and doubts.
3. Prepare to be challenged.
4. Practice personal spiritual disciplines.

> Compared to high school, I now know more about myself and less about what I believe than I used to. I hope this will resolve at some point in my life . . . at this point it's on hold because I don't have the time or the tools. It's hard to find time to think about religion or God, and college feels more like living from one day to the next and losing focus on big-picture things.
>
> —Conner

Sticky Faith Made Practical

The churches we worked with had a ton of intensely practical ideas that you might use in seeking to help the seniors you work with develop a faith that will stick as they leave your group. We've divided these strategies into three sections:

1. **Ongoing series or small groups**—like the senior breakfasts described at the beginning of this chapter.
2. **One-time events and rites of passage**—like a senior overnighter or ceremony
3. **Post-graduation ideas**—suggestions for what can be done after "Pomp and Circumstance" to help graduates survive, and even thrive, after they have moved on from youth group.

> As a follow-up to our research, we've also developed a *Sticky Faith Teen Curriculum: 10 Lessons to Nurture Faith Beyond High School* as part of this line of resources. You can learn more about it at www.stickyfaith.org.

Ongoing Series or Small Groups

Many churches and ministries have developed specific ways of engaging students in an ongoing way throughout their senior year, as these students prepare to conclude their time in high school and move on to the next stage of their journeys:

Monthly or Weekly Senior Gathering. This is probably the idea we've heard the most, with all kinds of variations on the theme. Set up a regular time during the students' senior year when they can meet together as a group for discussion, fellowship, and support. Later in this chapter you'll find a list of discussion topics that might be incorporated into these gatherings, either for a single session or in an ongoing way. (You'll find the list on pages 176 and 177). Here are a few other ideas and tips from youth workers for making these groups successful:

• Invite campus pastors and/or campus ministry leaders as well as previous graduates who have made it through their freshman year to speak to seniors. Include students with differing college experiences: both secular and Christian campuses, those who join fraternities or sororities and those who don't, those who get connected with churches or campus ministries and those who don't, etc.

- Include skill-building outings. One youth pastor we heard from takes seniors to a laundromat (yes, with their dirty laundry) and to a grocery store to shop for food on an imaginary budget.
- Start earlier. Rather than a brief series for a few weeks in the spring, many youth pastors now plan a yearlong series beginning in the fall of the senior year. Others start in the junior year with a two-year scope of lessons and transition strategy.
- Invite the senior pastor to one or more meetings, or even have dinner at his or her home with the whole group.
- Culminate the series with an overnighter or meaningful trip together (from camping to mission work to the beach).
- Host gender-separate groups for part or all of the series, focusing on some of the same issues while exploring special considerations that guys and girls need to make as they prepare for life after high school. For instance, how will they handle romantic relationships and sexual pressures in the midst of the college hookup scene? How do same-gender friendships for guys and for girls look different in college than they do in high school? What does it mean to be a man or woman of God, and how do gender roles they've learned or assumed in the past fit—or not—with their current understandings?

Mentoring Partnerships. One high school ministry we know pairs each high school senior with an adult from the congregation who can serve as a mentor, with the expectation that they will continue the mentoring relationship through at least the first year after high school. Another church is experimenting with connecting high school seniors with senior adults in the congregation in a "Senior to Senior" partnership. This could be set up either as short-term conversation partners or long-term mentors. Or, you could match each student with an adult in a vocational path the student hopes to pursue.

Church Visits. This may seem threatening or counterintuitive to some of us, but we've heard from youth workers who have found it really effective to expose seniors to other churches. Often this happens after graduation on Sundays throughout the summer. As students travel together to worship with different congregations and debrief afterward, they begin to think through what will be important to them as they search for new churches away from home. It also raises great questions about why churches and denominations are different and what those differences mean. You may want to study up on church history ahead of time! If you start this earlier in the year, you could also visit some college campus ministries.

As you visit different churches or college groups together, create a list of questions to help students process the experiences and think about what makes each church unique. The point is not to glamorize "church shopping," but to give them the tools to prayerfully and thoughtfully identify a church or college group that fits who they are and can help them develop Sticky Faith. Here's a start to that list:

1. What is the mission or vision of this group?
2. Where does this group meet? How am I going to get there?
3. When does this group meet? How does that fit into my schedule?
4. How many people are involved? Of those involved, how many people are my gender and/or year in school and/or ethnicity? What kind of diversity is present in the congregation? How important is it to be with folks who are the same or different in these ways?
5. Who leads this group? How do I connect with the leader(s)?
6. What's the teaching like? How about the worship?
7. Are there small groups or Bible studies that are part of this group?

8. What does this group do to reach out to people who don't know Jesus yet?
9. What does this group do to help those who are poor or marginalized?
10. How can I use my gifts and talents as part of this group?

When we asked college students what criteria were most important to them in choosing a church, these were their top five:
1. the teaching
2. the mission/vision
3. the leaders
4. the worship
5. outreach to people in need

College Tours. Some youth leaders make it a point to take students on tours of one or more college campuses. One youth pastor told us he does this in the fall. He intentionally visits campuses where his youth group graduates are now freshmen, so the group can visit with those alums to encourage and learn from them. While you're at it, take the opportunity to visit a local church near each campus, too.

Transition into Adult Small Groups. To give students more of a taste for the full church and their place in it as emerging adults, consider placing seniors (in pairs or triplets, so they feel less isolated) in your church's adult small groups. This may require some training, both for the small group leaders and the seniors!

Transition into Leadership. Some youth pastors move seniors into leadership positions in middle school or elementary ministry, helping them see themselves as important contributors to the faith of younger kids. This usually works best when students are teamed with and supported by adult leaders as they serve.

Involve Parents. Part of the senior prep may include preparing the parents for the coming transition. You may host a simultaneous parents-of-seniors small group during one or more meetings of your series (perhaps led by parents who have already crossed the transition beyond high school with their own kids) or a workshop or prayer night for parents. One youth worker gathers parents and kids together for a joint meeting. She asks parents to make a list of what they think their kids need to know before they leave home, while students make a list of what they think they need to know. Then they share their lists and have rich conversation about the similarities and differences.

> Never let a kid leave for college without a few leads for potential churches or campus ministries to check out. For help connecting with other incoming Christian freshmen and learning about campus ministries, point students to www.LiveAbove.com, hosted by the Youth Transition Network.

One-time Events and Rites of Passage

Recently I (Brad) had the opportunity to speak to a group of students who'd just graduated from high school and were heading out on a senior trip with their youth pastor. As I prepared for that session, I couldn't help but think about my own post-graduation summer more than 15 years ago.

I remember my excitement and anxiety about leaving for college. I remember there were a lot of "lasts" with my friends. And I remember some "firsts." That summer I went on my first road trip without my parents or other adults. I also went on my first mission trip.

A small group from my little church learned a cheesy Christian musical and went to the hills of Kentucky to perform it in the evenings at a series of churches. During the days, we painted and renovated a church playground and served at a rural mission. It wasn't a glamorous trip, but that experience shaped me. It shaped my perceptions of poverty. It shaped my understanding of God. It shaped a new belief in the significance of prioritizing serving others over building my resume for professional success.

The summer after graduation is significant in part because it's such a liminal (or "in-between") period of time. You've left one world, but you're not quite yet in another. So by very definition (of anthropologists, anyway[3]), you are in a liminal period—standing on a threshold, having largely stepped away from your old identity, but just starting to open the door to your next stage of life and new identity. High school graduates know on some level that this is happening, but often have very little guidance regarding how to live in the in-between world or how to step through the door into post-high-school adulthood.

Helping to give shape and meaning to the in-between, as well as guidance for stepping into the new identity, is one of the primary functions of the rites of passage described below. Churches are incredibly important communities for utilizing rites of passage, and there are multiple points during the senior year or post-graduation summer that offer opportunities to tap into this season of passage.

> For more ideas on creating rites of passage in youth ministry, see www.stickyfaith.org.

Senior Barak. Barak (pronounced "bu-ROCK") is the Hebrew word for "bless," and my church holds a yearly tradition of a *Barak* night for friends, family, and youth leaders to intentionally bless graduating seniors. Each student's parents are given an information sheet about a month prior to the event, including instructions for writing a letter of blessing to their child. At the event, parents read their letters aloud in front of the group. Then other students, leaders, and family have opportunities to share. Many students find it to be an important time of affirmation. As one student reflected this year, "Usually it's hard to get encouragement from my dad, so to hear him read a letter to me was powerful."

> To download a sample instruction sheet that you can give to parents in preparation for a senior *Barak*, visit www.stickyfaith.org.

All-Church Worship Services. We've already mentioned that many churches have some kind of "Senior Sunday" recognition service. Sometimes this consists of parading students across the platform and giving them Bibles. Other times there's more involved. Here are a few ideas we've picked up:

- Invite seniors to share with the congregation not just where they're headed next, but also their stories of faith and the ways they've been shaped by the congregation and youth ministry.
- Allow seniors to take over the service—crafting and leading the worship, and sharing the teaching. If it is acceptable in your context, empower seniors to serve communion elements to the congregation.
- Incorporate ritual acts of blessing where the congregation speaks a blessing liturgy and/or lays hands on students in prayer.
- Publicly acknowledge and pray (as a congregation) for seniors at the beginning AND end of their senior year. The beginning of the year can serve as a commissioning for the transitional period ahead of them, and the end of the year can be a time of conferring adulthood and commissioning for service.
- Involve seniors' parents by inviting them to the platform to pray for their children, or giving them a chance to publicly share advice they would give to parents of younger children. Mentors, small group leaders, and other significant adults from the church could also join in this time, surrounding students with prayer.
- Collect (perhaps with the help of parents, long-term volunteers, and/or other students) photographs of seniors from throughout their entire time of involvement in the youth ministry, and create photo albums to give to the graduates. These albums can be great reminders of the stories students have shared during their journeys in the community of faith.

All-Day or Multi-Day Rite-of-Passage Events. If you have the opportunity and resources to take seniors or recent grads away on a day or overnight (or longer) trip, build in more than just fun. Take advantage of extended time together to bless them, allow them to reflect on their journeys through journaling and sharing with others, and maybe even present them with a significant challenge like a solo wilderness experience. One church shared that they have rite-of-passage events for guys and girls separately, where staff and volunteers collaborate to create top-20 lists of tips for college. Their collective wisdom is both personal and priceless. An East Coast youth pastor told us the seniors from his church go on a summer mission trip after graduation, joined by both the youth pastor and the college pastor. That way, youth group graduates forge new relationships with the college pastor in the context of serving others.

Topics Seniors Need to Discuss

Okay, so once you have a plan for the kind of one-time or ongoing events you'll host in order to prepare seniors for the future, then you're faced with another question: What are you going to talk about? The list below includes (in no particular order) ideas based on research, think tanks, and feedback from youth pastors across the country. Use this list to get thinking about what your seniors need to discuss:

- Finding a new church and campus ministry
- Finding new friends, especially new Christian relationships
- Navigating old friendships that often change rapidly after high school
- Planning for the first two weeks of college, especially choices about parties, alcohol, and sex
- Recovering if you stumble, fall down, or run the other way from Christ
- Managing time
- Managing money
- Handling emerging doubts and questions about faith
- Engaging your changing view of God, yourself, and others
- Staying in touch with adults from your home church
- Finding new mentors
- Managing changing relationships with parents and other family members

- Practicing faith in college (spiritual disciplines and other forms of engagement)
- Exploring and building your faith identity, as opposed to lock-boxing your faith away (see chapter 3)
- Having conversations with students from other faiths and worldviews
- Recognizing and using your gifts and talents to serve others
- Discerning your calling and vocation
- Living missionally on the college campus and in adult life
- Developing your critical thinking and decision-making skills
- Understanding the true gospel (chapter 2) and living under God's grace
- Preparing for dating relationships in college
- Preparing for the possibility of finding a long-term marriage partner during or after college
- Experiencing loss

One of the hallmarks of the freshman experience is loss, but this feeling often surprises students. Help prepare students for losses they may face by talking through the following types of loss:

1. *Material Loss*—"Yes, you can grieve if you lose your cell phone."
2. *Relationship Loss*—"Yes, you can grieve if you break up with your boyfriend."
3. *Intrapsychic Loss or Loss of a Dream*—"Yes, you can grieve not getting the job you wanted."
4. *Functional Loss*—"Yes, you can grieve breaking your arm."
5. *Role Loss*—"Yes, you can grieve being single if you get married."
6. *Systemic Loss*—"Yes, you can grieve when you leave home and your entire network of supportive relationships to go away to school."[4]

For more resources on grief and loss, see www.stickyfaith.org.

Post-Graduation Ideas

Amid all we learned from the students we studied, one of the themes that painfully emerged from the interviews was that students felt abandoned by youth leaders after graduation. Students felt sad and even angry when youth leaders failed to contact them. We could reprint pages of stories from students who never received a single call, letter, or text from a youth pastor or volunteer. To the left is just one example:

Even students who were involved in ministry leadership and had considered the youth ministry staff to be close friends often felt completely ignored once they graduated from the ministry. Some even mentioned that they ended up in college with older students who had been on the youth ministry team, and suddenly these leaders weren't as excited to see them on campus as they were at youth group.

To prevent that abandonment, churches have shared a number of strategies for post-graduation engagement that help keep students connected to the body of Christ whether they're living two or two hundred miles away.

> I graduated and went off to college, and I didn't hear back from those people in the youth ministry again. They didn't make any effort to stay in touch. So that was kind of disappointing. No one ever sent me an email saying, "How's school going?" and "What's up? You should come visit us." Or anything like that. It kind of felt sad, you know? I knew these people, they were my friends, and then I didn't hear from them. And I understand people are busy, and I was busy with school, and the leaders especially are busy with their families and other groups and stuff. But it would have been nice to have a little bit more follow-through. It would have felt more sincere.
> —Brody

Ongoing Mentoring Relationships. As we mentioned above, some churches are trying to establish mentoring relationships during high school that last into the college years, or at least the first few months after graduation. Whether you continue on or start fresh, the important thing is to connect young adults with mature adults who can accompany them on their spiritual journey during this transition time.

> The Evangelical Covenant denomination has created a free mentoring guide for young adults and their mentors called *The Real Life Field Guide*. It invites topical discussions framed in the context of spiritual conversation and anchored in scriptural reflection, and it includes a companion mentoring manual. You can download it for free at www.covchurch.org/resources/real-life-field-guide.

My first year in college, I got like two, maybe four mailings from my home church. Of course I'm a college student, and so the things I value are food, food, and possibly money, right? So I get these mailings from my church where I spent 18 years, and it's those devotional booklets that all the old people love to read but teenagers would never pick up in their whole life. They're mailing those to college students, and I'm like, "Uh thanks, I don't know what I'm supposed to do with this." And aside from that, there wasn't anyone who was trying to keep in contact at all.

—Jeff

On-Campus Gatherings. Often, a number of students from a particular congregation will attend the same nearby university. If that's the case with your graduates, consider hosting an on-campus gathering for new college freshmen sometime during the first couple of weeks—a check-in, encouragement, we're-cheering-you-on kind of meeting. You might even recruit volunteers who can make this an ongoing ministry to college students from your church.

Intentional, Regular Contact. From youth group care packages to "adopt-a-college-student" programs, congregations that make an effort to stay in contact with college students in an ongoing way make a real difference in those students' college experiences, especially during freshman year. In addition to remembering to send an occasional "What's up?" text just to check in, we must help students by putting a plan in place to keep consistent contact with them alive.

One creative church devotes an entire Wednesday evening youth group meeting in the fall to baking cookies and writing notes to recent graduates. Not only are alums reminded that their church still cares about them, but the high school students making the care packages learn they won't be forgotten after they graduate. Another church spends the first 10 minutes of a meeting near the end of each semester passing around encouragement cards that get mailed to college students before finals week.

Maximize Social Networking Channels. Online social media is part of your students' communication DNA. Tap into the potential of popular networks to stay connected with students, whether that's through posting messages on their profiles or creating alum groups for your youth ministry.

For more ideas about maintaining contact with grads,
see www.stickyfaith.org.

Holiday Parties. Take advantage of the natural windows of time during which recent graduates tend to return home, especially the first Thanksgiving and Christmas breaks. Many youth ministries host parties during these times as a casual way to gather recent youth group graduates so they can reconnect, share stories, and perhaps worship and pray together. It can be a great opportunity to encourage any students who are struggling and also to communicate that the church will continue to welcome them whenever they're home.

Spring Break or Summer Gatherings. Similarly, gatherings during spring break or summer vacation can also help students reconnect with one another, with you, and maybe even with God.

Engage Adult Small Groups. One student we interviewed spoke of how adult small groups from her home church have taken it upon themselves to minister to college students. They send cards, care packages, and prayers. She relates, "I know they're thinking about us and praying for us because they tell me every time I come home. It's had a big impact on me, and also on my non-Christian roommates."

For Those Who Stay

Some of the students we serve do NOT move away to college or the military after high school. They stay home, perhaps attending community college or entering the workforce (or both, or neither). Sometimes these graduates of our youth groups struggle even more because their lives remain more static while their friends move away and have exciting new experiences. In our eagerness to care for those who move on, we also need to be careful to consider the special needs of those who stay behind.

To help these students develop their own Sticky Faith, you might want to try the following:

- If your church has a college or young-adult ministry these students will be joining, commit to attend the first few gatherings of that group during the summer or fall, and let your students know you will be there.
- If your church doesn't have a post-high-school ministry, help graduates get connected into adult groups and places to serve if they are not connected already.
- When possible, drop by your students' workplaces, campuses, or homes, just to let them know you were thinking of them.
- Recruit volunteers who intentionally mentor students who stay close to home.

Letters from College

In our surveys and interviews, we asked college students to think back from their current vantage point of three or four years out and consider what they would say to the current crop of high school seniors preparing for the transition. Some of their responses are scattered throughout this book, but we pulled together a few particularly powerful quotes to share as we close this chapter. You may want to read some of these thoughts to your seniors, or invite graduates from your own ministry to write similar letters from college.

- "I would tell them to prepare, to plan ahead. When you go away to college, you don't just say, 'I'm going to leave, I want to go here,' and just pack your bag and go. You learn about it, you find out what the environment is going to be like, if you're going to need furniture in your dorm, and what kind of clothes you're going to need to prepare for the weather. If you're going to do that amount of preparing for moving, your faith needs the same kind of preparation. Look into what the college environment is going to provide for you positively, and maybe expose you to negatively, and prepare for all of that. Know your faith and be willing and strong enough to let it be challenged."
- "College is one of the neatest times to be bold enough to share your faith because I think the potential for impact on a college campus is enormous."
- "It's easy to be naive and think that because you were a strong Christian and knew what you believed and why you believed it in high school, that it's going to be the same in college. It's not! In high school I had a great community, but coming to college is so testing. And man, it can be so lonely that you start to question everything. So get plugged in with people who care about you, at all levels. That would have been so helpful for me, and I don't think I would be feeling so lost about stuff right now."
- "It's okay to go through periods of doubt and distrust and disillusionment. It's okay to go through periods of questioning and confusion. Don't run away from them. At the same time, don't go off the deep end. Do the intellectual and spiritual soul searching within the context of a secure community of people who truly love you."

- "If anyone is going into college saying, 'I want to know how best to honor God in this situation that I'm going into,' they can succeed. I don't think that anyone who goes through life looking for opportunities to honor God will be left hanging. I think God is faithful to answer that and to say, 'You're looking for me, and I'm going to reveal myself to you.'"

sticky discussion questions

1. How would you describe your current plan for preparing seniors for life after youth group?

2. After reading this chapter, what ideas do you think are already represented in your plan, and what new ideas could you use to bolster or revise your plan?

3. On a scale of 1 to 5, how equipped is your ministry to help prepare seniors for the transition? If your score is pretty low, what resources might increase your ministry team's ability to support students through the transition to college?

4. What people in your church could help you strategize and develop support for students after they graduate from high school? Who will you contact this week to get the conversation going?

5. Can you personally write down the names of three to five seniors whom you can invest in for the next two to three years across the transition? Who are they?

9

the path to sticky change

As a youth pastor, I generally feel empowered to make changes within the youth ministry, as needed, without too much drama. But making changes that involve a church-wide philosophical perspective has proven to be much more difficult! I have found that making small changes on the ground level has been much more effective than giving a presentation at a pastors' meeting regarding why we should change. Our youth team has partnered with other departments (like college and young adults) in bringing about change within our ministries that we hope will lead to larger changes in the future. In fact, the word change can be very divisive, so I've replaced it in my vocabulary with things like "moving forward" or "joining God where he is at work."
—Juaneta, youth pastor

During our process of change, one thing that became clear to us was that change is like trying to teach a pubescent junior high boy how to dance; an art that required us to have patience, perseverance, and persistence. Even through the awkward fumbling around together and maybe some bruised toes, we somehow managed to see the dance as not merely a means to an end, but rather an opportunity for us to experience the movement of the Spirit in and through us, bringing us closer and deeper together in unity.
—Henry, director of student ministries

"Insanity is doing the same thing over and over again and expecting different results." This quotation, usually attributed to Albert Einstein, should be plastered over your desk and recited at the start of every one of your leadership meetings. It should also be written in BIG, **bold** letters across the top of your Sticky Faith brainstorming notes.

As we've presented the results of our research in churches across the nation, we've found that very few youth leaders and parents object to the Sticky Faith findings, or even the practical implications they suggest. Instead, they generally nod their heads in agreement, since our discoveries echo their own theology, intuition, and experiences.

Yet even as leaders and parents nod in agreement, they are often simultaneously scratching their heads, burdened by a new question: How do we move toward a new, stickier approach to youth ministry? Whether we're having coffee with one youth leader or teaching a seminar for hundreds, our discussions quickly move from WHAT needs to change to HOW do we bring about change, both in our youth ministries and in our churches.

Note the final eight words of the last paragraph: in our youth ministries *and in our churches.*

The reality is that Sticky Faith isn't just a youth ministry issue. It's a whole church issue.

This truth became even clearer to us during our Sticky Faith Learning Cohorts. As we've already described, FYI walked through a 12-month Sticky Faith journey with 12 churches committed to live out Sticky Faith together and individually. We then repeated this process with 16 more churches for a second year. After the early miles of wading through our research, we quickly realized that this wasn't just about our youth ministries. We couldn't reach our destination of a Sticky Gospel, a Sticky Church, or Sticky Families if our congregations weren't walking with us.

Let's be honest: The average congregation isn't looking to the youth pastor to be their trail guide. Sure, we youth leaders are fun to have along, and we are great at keeping people smiling and laughing during the hike; but we're not usually the ones out front, blazing the path.

Thanks in large part to the expertise of Dr. Scott Cormode, the Hugh De Pree Professor of Leadership Development at Fuller Seminary, we were able to wrestle with the question of *How do I help my whole church engage in Sticky Faith?* and actually pin down some answers. While it's impossible to capture our entire 12-month journey, we couldn't end this book without sharing some ideas from Scott and others, as well as a few tools that we found to be indispensable in navigating the path to Sticky Faith.

The Power of Story

The most important guiding principle—the true north of our journey—was the power of story. In fact, under the coaching of Scott Cormode, we learned that vision cannot be separated from story because Scott defines *vision* as a "shared story of future hope."[1]

A shared story. Of future hope.

As powerful as research is, stories are more powerful. Stories are more memorable, more personal, and more transformative.

As your church is navigating its own path to Sticky Faith, try asking two fundamental questions:

1. *What stories of real-life people in your ministry or church already capture your Sticky Faith vision?*
2. *If you could imagine stories that capture how you hope God builds Sticky Faith, what would they be?*

Stories of God at Work Today

The first of these two questions invites you and your church to consider how the Sticky Faith you envision is a natural outgrowth of what God is already doing in your midst. Where are you already seeing Sticky Faith incarnated?

One of the primary Sticky Faith change areas for many of the churches in our yearlong journey was to move toward a more intergenerational approach to ministry. So one of those churches answered question number one by talking about Leo and Trevor.

As a teenager, Leo had been heavily involved in gangs before he

187

met the Lord. Now he's a 40-year-old dad of two teenagers who also serves as an usher at his church. As Leo saw kids walking into the worship service every Sunday, he was drawn to Trevor, a high school kid Leo later described as a carbon copy of himself as a teenager.

Leo contacted the youth pastor and asked how Trevor was doing. Upon hearing that Trevor was flirting with gang-like behaviors, Leo asked the youth pastor if it would be good for him to invite Trevor to join Leo and his family for a day in the mountains to play in the snow. The youth pastor couldn't say quickly enough, "Definitely."

Trevor did go with Leo's family, and the two guys formed a bond. Leo was able to share about his own past and point out warning signs he saw in Trevor's life.

Thanks in no small part to Leo, Trevor started to move away from his gang. But as he began to distance himself from the gang, Trevor received threats against his life. Trevor started carrying a gun to school for self-defense.

Recently, school officials found the gun, and Trevor was arrested for carrying a concealed weapon. Trevor has a legitimate self-defense claim, and guess who is walking through the process with Trevor, attending every court hearing, and offering support in between? You guessed it: Leo.

For this church that already wants to head toward intergenerational ministry, Leo and Trevor are a narrative snapshot of their hopes for the future. The story of their relationship affirms the good work God is already doing and stretches the entire church toward a stickier, more intergenerational future.

The churches in our Sticky Faith Learning Cohorts found the greatest success in writing their stories when they . . .

- Invited others from their ministry and church to join in the brainstorming and writing process
- Developed a few ministry values or goals as driving forces for the story
- Were as specific as possible in describing people in the story, often basing their characters on real-life people

---

Stories of Your Hope for the Future

If the first question allows you to pinpoint how God is already working, Scott Cormode's second question allows you to prayerfully dream about the future God has for you. When asked to share a story that described where they wanted to be in two years, one church in the Midwest spoke of their desire to give young people the space to ask hard questions and wrestle with their doubts.

> In her sophomore year of college, Koly knows it's time to choose a major. In light of the good and bad advice from parents, friends, advisors, and former small group leaders, Koly makes this choice based on the identity she's discovered over the past two years. She sees this as a new opportunity to ask Who am I? and to discover more by asking Who is God? She chooses engineering because, seeing God as a Creator in whose image she's made, she wants to use her creativity to design a new cement that resists potholes in the harsh Michigan winters.

Upon hearing this story, this entire congregation can now clearly picture Koly and the importance of stretching her with hard questions before she graduates from high school. And folks who live in a snowy climate can also celebrate Koly's soon-to-be-invented pothole-proof cement!

The Power of Shared Stories

Once you know your Sticky Faith stories, you share them. Often. And broadly. Because the power of the story lies not in the story itself, but in the story as it is shared.

The next time you have an opportunity to share with your entire church about your short-term mission trip, make sure you share stories that capture the dreams you have for your church. Instead of sharing only about how great it was to see teenagers interact with children at the Guatemalan orphanage, take a few minutes to share about how the parents who went on the trip loved sharing the experience with their own kids.

When you're meeting with parents who are new to the church,

instead of talking about the fun of the annual amusement park weekend, paint a picture of the way this weekend helps adult leaders and kids have a shared experience, an experience that helps them feel more connected in future small group discussions.

The next time you're asked to give an update about youth group at your church business meeting or the women's Bible study, instead of mentioning your decked-out snack bar, talk about the kid who shared on Sunday about his anger at God because of his parents' divorce, and how your youth ministry is now walking through this time of doubt, struggle, and growth with him.

As the youth leaders who have journeyed with us have discovered, you have more power than you think to bring about change through the stories you tell.

That's so important we are going to say it again: *You have more power than you think to bring about change through the stories you tell.*

Build a Sticky Faith Team

As is probably apparent to you already, changing your church is a job that is . . . well . . . bigger than you can accomplish on your own. So you need a team—a team of strategically invited people who are either already onboard the Sticky Faith train or who you feel you should get onboard before the train leaves the station.

Odds are good this team will include the pastor or volunteer leaders who work most closely with the children in your church. We are more and more convinced that families and kids have often been profoundly shaped by the children's ministry before they even walk into our youth ministries. We inherit the good, the bad, and the ugly of our children's ministry and the imprint it leaves on kids and families.

Several of the 28 Sticky Faith Learning Cohort churches made dramatic changes in their children's ministry curriculum—changes that brought about greater ownership and partnership with parents. One of these churches even shifted its entire children's Sunday school approach so that parents and stepparents are expected to talk with their kids about the lesson *before* Sunday morning. The Sunday morning discussion is geared to be a reinforcement of what kids have already discussed with their parents. Parents are learning that they are the primary spiritual nurturers of their children, and they are learning that before they even get to the youth ministry.

Your Sticky Faith team might include your worship leader, your adult Sunday school coordinator, your missions chair, your senior pastor, and maybe even a few key students. You'll probably want to invite parents into the mix, as well as some of your most committed adult volunteers.

You might be the quarterback, but even the best quarterback needs a team. Otherwise you will never reach the end zone.

What Do You Do with Your Team?

While building a Sticky Faith team might seem difficult, your greatest challenge comes after you have your team all set: What do you do with it?

Our 28 churches made the most progress toward Sticky Faith when they were able to do what Harvard's Ronald Heifetz describes as maintaining "disciplined attention."[2] By maintaining disciplined attention, they were able to focus on their Sticky Faith goals instead of slipping into old patterns and paradigms. Often that meant eliminating any program or energy-suck that didn't nudge them toward their Sticky Faith goals.

Most of the churches sought to maintain disciplined attention by holding monthly or semi-monthly Sticky Faith team meetings. The main purposes of these meetings were to:

1. Pray.
2. Tell new stories—stories that could be shared—that reflected the Sticky Faith vision.
3. Report on work done since the last meeting.
4. Assign tasks with deadlines to specific individuals who were expected to report at the next Sticky Faith team meeting.
5. Evaluate the momentum and pace of the change. When it

was too fast and furious, they would turn down the heat.

When it was too slow and safe, they turned it up a notch.

Josh Kerkhoff, the Next Generation pastor at Solana Beach Presbyterian Church and a member of our first Sticky Faith Learning Cohort, found enormous value in his Sticky Faith team's regular meetings. Josh reports, "In our times together, we have shared personal and ministry stories and have taken a step back from our day-to-day responsibilities to look at the big picture of our church and what impact our church has on kids, students, and their families. We initially didn't know what would come of our regular meetings but have found that our bimonthly meetings have been vital to our relationships, our vision, and a shared future direction that God is moving us toward."

Identify Advocates and Obstacles

Scott Cormode reminded the churches in our cohorts that change almost always leads to two reactions within a group. On the one hand, there will be people who love it. On the other hand, there will be people who hate it. Odds are good that even before you make the change, you can identify the folks who are most likely to love it, as well as those who are most likely to hate it.

The first group is, obviously, easier to know how to handle. If we give them some idea of what's going on, they can be champions for these new ideas and share their enthusiasm with others.

The second group is much more challenging. So most of us try to avoid them and hope they'll go away.

They never do.

Based on the work of William Ury, Senior Fellow in the Harvard Negotiation Project, the youth pastors in the learning cohorts were coached in two primary strategies that can help us sidestep the common pitfalls that often trip us up when we face conflict with others.[3]

1. Instead of arguing, try to understand.

We often make the mistake of approaching conflict with one overriding goal: Convince the other person to change his position. When we start with this goal, we normally accomplish the opposite: The other person ends up even more entrenched in his position. As a bonus, so do we.

We would be wise to learn from the wisdom of Abraham Lincoln, a leader who by any account brought about major, sticky changes. President Lincoln is reported to have said, "When I am getting ready to reason with a man, I spend one-third of my time thinking about myself and what I am going to say and two-thirds about him and what he is going to say." Even prior to meeting with a person, Lincoln adopted the posture of understanding, not arguing.

When you actually have the chance to meet and you have heard the other person's concerns and frustrations, Scott Cormode recommends responding to those thoughts as neutrally as possible, "I really want to make sure I understand you on your terms. I think what you are saying is . . ." and then summarize that person's words without any interpretation. When you have finished summarizing, ask, "Is that right?" Not only do you want to understand, but you also want to make sure that the other individual believes that you understand.

2. Instead of blocking, try to build a golden bridge of agreement.
Your goal is not victory; your goal is a mutually satisfactory solution. Often the only obstacle preventing two people from reaching agreement is each person's fear of losing face. You can reach a mutual agreement if you help the other person get something she wants, or if you pursue one of her ideas (even if you somewhat reframe it) so you are moving together in the same direction. Look for common ground and see if you can show how your Sticky Faith changes will, in fact, help accomplish the other person's goals as well.

> For more on how to handle conflict in your church,
> see www.stickyfaith.org.

Communicate, Communicate, Communicate

If we've sent out an email announcing a change, we tend to assume that every kid, parent, and leader has read it, understands it, and remembers it. But we end up surprised when we then make the change we announced in the email, and two-thirds of the folks most affected by it are shocked that anything new is happening.

Given how busy kids, parents, and leaders are today, it's almost impossible to overcommunicate with them. Whether it's a weekly email blast, regular parent meetings, or specially trained carrier pigeons, add up whatever communication you think needs to happen about the Sticky Faith changes you will be making. Now double it. At this point, you have a better estimation of the communication that needs to happen in order for the change to be successful.

In your newly doubled communication efforts, be as encouraging as possible. Share both Sticky Faith research and Sticky Faith stories. Describe prayer requests that reflect your Sticky Faith goals. Invite folks to contact you if they have any questions or comments. When they do get in touch with you, use those opportunities to build up your story-telling and encouragement muscles.

Experiment Around the Margins

While some churches may quickly develop strong momentum toward Sticky Faith and can charge ahead, most churches need to take more time. Your ultimate goal is systemic change, but odds are good that you need to take the first three to six months to "experiment around the margins" with your Sticky Faith changes.[4] In other words, try piloting your new ideas with one particular small group, or one grade of kids, or one handful of families. When things go well, identify those signs of hope and nurture them so they grow bigger. Capture those stories and practice telling them to different audiences.

It's often during the early experiments that you first identify both your greatest cheerleaders and your greatest naysayers. Because your initial steps have been made on a smaller scale, you have plenty of time to respond to both groups (as described above) before you really hit your Sticky Faith stride.

Anchor the Sticky Faith Changes in Your Culture

Your hope is that the Sticky Faith approach to kids will weave its way through, and wrap its way around, your ministry and your church. As Harvard professor John P. Kotter has stated, "In the final analysis, change sticks when it becomes 'the way we do things around here.'"[5]

In his study of organizational change, Kotter has identified two factors common to organizations that anchor changes in their corporate cultures. The first factor is a conscious attempt to show how the new approaches, behaviors, and attitudes have helped improve performance. In Sticky Faith parlance, that means showing how kids' relationships with Jesus, with one another, with their families, and with the church are strengthened—both now and hopefully in the future.

The way to show results is through communication. As we said before, you have more power than you think to bring about change through the stories you tell. Tell real stories of real kids with real Sticky Faith, and you'll get more real change.

Secondly, Kotter has seen the importance of taking sufficient time to make sure the next generation of management really does personify the new approach. As Kotter warns, "One bad succession decision at the top of an organization can undermine a decade of hard work."[6] Our Sticky Faith Learning Cohorts made the most progress when as many paid and volunteer leaders as possible were all on board and headed in the same direction.

Be Patient. Good Things Take Time.

Earlier we asked you to add up how much communication you think will be needed to explain your Sticky Faith changes and then double that amount for a more accurate estimation.

You need to do the same thing with the amount of time you think it will take.

But bit by bit, story by story, kid by kid, prayer by prayer, God will develop Sticky Faith. Pretty soon it will become your new normal. Along the way, you and your team will get to experience one of the greatest joys possible: seeing kids stick not just to you, or even to one another or to your church, but to the Lord Jesus Christ.

sticky discussion questions

1. On a scale of 1 to 10 (with 10 being "very much"), how much do you like the definition of *vision* as a "shared story of future hope"? If you scored an 8 or higher, what do you like about it? If you scored a 7 or less, what should be different about a definition of *vision*?

2. What stories of real-life people in your ministry or church already embody the Sticky Faith vision?

3. If you could imagine stories that capture how you hope God builds kids' faith, what would they be?

4. What other adults (and maybe even kids) can you invite to be part of your Sticky Faith team? When can you connect with them? If you were to start meeting with that team regularly, what would you do to maintain disciplined attention?

5. What are your five best ideas for how to communicate about your desired changes?

Appendix

the college transition project: research overview

The Fuller Youth Insititute's College Transition Project is comprised of four separate research initiatives: an initial quantitative pilot study involving 69 youth group graduates; two three-year longitudinal (primarily quantitative) studies of high school seniors during their first three years in college, involving 162 and 227 students respectively; and qualitative interviews with 45 former youth group graduates between two and four years beyond high school graduation.

In 2004, the Fuller Youth Institute (FYI), at that time known as the Center for Youth and Family Ministry, initiated a pilot research study called the College Transition Project (CTP), surveying a group of 69 college students who were alumni of a single youth group in the Northwest. The preliminary results suggested a link between a college student's current spiritual state and the quality of key relationships during the high school years, including the youth group environment itself.

As a result, in 2005–2006 FYI launched a broader study, recruiting students involved in church youth groups during the spring of their high school senior year. To participate in the survey, students were required to be 18 years of age or older, part of a church youth group, and intending to attend a college or university upon graduation. Students were recruited through FYI's nationwide network of youth leader contacts, resulting in a sample of 162 students who were surveyed four times over three years. Thirty of these students participated in subsequent one-hour interviews during their fourth year out of high school.

In 2006–07, with the support of funding from the Lilly Endowment, FYI launched another nationwide longitudinal study of high school seniors connected to church youth groups to examine their experiences at five points: the spring of their senior year in high school (2007), the fall and spring of their first year in college (2007–2008), the spring of their second year in college (2009), and the spring of their third year in college (2010). The primary goal of the study was to determine if there are programmatic and relational characteristics of high school youth ministries and churches that have a demonstrable relationship to how students make the faith adjustment to life beyond high school.

With support from another private foundation, Dr. Cheryl Crawford conducted two-hour qualitative interviews with 15 college students who had been part of a leadership development program at a Christian camp during high school. These interviews were conducted during spring semester of the freshman year of college. She subsequently interviewed the same students the following spring.

Participants

The sample for this longitudinal study launched in 2007 consisted of 227 high school seniors drawn from different regions across the United States. More than half (56.3 percent) of the respondents were female while 43.7 percent were male. The sample was predominantly White/Caucasian (78.0 percent). Asian/Asian American students comprised 11.0 percent of the sample, while Hispanic/Latino students accounted for 5.0 percent. African-American and Native American students each accounted for 1.4 percent of the sample. Participants reported a median grade point average of 3.5 to 3.99, with 63 percent of the sample having GPAs above 3.5. Given that 88 percent of seniors who apply to college have a GPA over 3.0, our sample represents a high-achieving group.[1] The majority of the participants came from larger churches. The median youth group size was 51-100 students, while the median church size was reported to be over 800 members.

Participants were mostly from intact families, with 83.8 percent reporting that they lived with both their father and mother; another 4.1 percent lived with a parent and stepparent. Overall, the parents of the participants were well educated; more than two-thirds (69.7 percent) of the mothers and nearly three-quarters of the fathers (73.0 percent) held at least a college degree. By far the majority of the fathers (88.2 percent) of the participants were employed full time, while fewer than half of the mothers were (42.5 percent).

Procedure

From October 2006 to February 2007, members of the research team who had developed networks in four geographical regions of the United States (the Southwest, the Northwest, the Southeast, and the Northeast) identified churches representing size, denominational, socioeconomic, and ethnic diversity. For this study, only churches employing full-time youth pastors were recruited. From March to June 2007, the youth ministry staff of each participating church was asked to invite senior students involved in their youth ministries to participate in the study. As with the pilot, students were eligible only if they were 18 years old or over and intended to attend a college upon graduation.

Students who agreed to participate in the study could do so in one of three ways: They could complete a paper-and-pencil version of the survey together (facilitated either by their youth pastor or a member of the FYI research team); they could complete a paper version of the survey individually at a time and place convenient to them; or they could complete an online version of the survey. In addition to the survey, each student was required to complete a consent form assuring confidentiality. Signed consent forms also contained an identification code that was unique to each individual, as well as contact information (i.e., an email address and a physical address) in order to track each student for future waves of data collection. All future data collection was done via online surveys.

Instruments

Faith Measures

Five measures of faith development were employed in order to create a composite picture of both internalized and externalized faith commitments and behaviors. For four of the measures, participants are asked to rate their agreement with each item on a five-point scale, ranging from *strongly disagree* (1) to *strongly agree* (5). The Intrinsic Religious Motivation scale[2] is comprised of 10 items measuring the extent to which an individual's religiosity is not simply external and behavioral, but internalized in terms of one's values and motivations. Sample items include, "My faith involves all of my life," and "I try hard to carry my religion over into all my other dealings in life." A similar measure, the Narrative Faith Relevance Scale,[3] assesses the extent to which one's decisions are influenced by the sense of having a relationship to God. Sample items include, "If and when I date someone, it is (or would be) important to me that God be pleased with the relationship," and "In choosing what college to attend, it is important to me to seek God's will." The third measure is the 17-item short form of the Search Institute's Faith Maturity Scale,[4] including items like "My faith shapes how I think and act each and every day," and "My life is committed to Jesus Christ." And the fourth is the Religious Support Scale,[5] assessing the extent to which participants feel supported and nurtured by God. Using social support items, the scale incorporates indicators such as "I am valued by God."

The fifth measure is a measure of religious behavior created for the CTP pilot. Ten items assess the frequency of engagement in a variety of corporate and individual behaviors, including such items as "pray alone," "read your Bible by yourself," and "attend a worship service or church-related event." Responses are given on a six-point scale, ranging from *less than once a month* (1) to *once a day or more* (6).

Youth Group Experience Measures

Three sets of items were created from qualitative data from earlier stages of the project in order to assess students' participation in and attitudes toward their youth group experience. First, students were asked about the frequency of participation in eight items over the past two months or the past year, including activities like retreats, mission trips, and midweek youth group. Second, participants were presented with 22 statements representing why students go to youth group, including, "It's where my friends are," and "I learn about God there." Students were asked to rate how true each statement was for them using a five-point scale ranging from *not true at all* (1) to *completely true* (5). Third, students were asked what they would want to see more or less of in their youth group. Thirteen items were presented, such as "one-on-one time with leaders" and "mission trips." Participants responded on a five-point scale ranging from *much less* (1) to *much more* (5).

Other Measures

In addition to these faith and youth ministry measures, other scales and questions were added related to perceived social support, parental support, support within the youth ministry, loneliness, extraversion, social desirability (as a control factor), and risk behaviors (sexual contact, alcohol use, and pornography use). Subsequent waves of data collection have included most of these same measures (particularly faith measures), in addition to scales and questions related to religious behaviors in college, the college spiritual environment, adjustment to college, doubts about faith, parental and other adult contact in college, parental faith discussions, preparation for decision making, and college participation in church and campus ministry.

The following are some of the spirituality instruments and their corresponding items.

Intrinsic Religious Motivation (Hoge, 1972)

1. My faith involves all of my life.
2. One should seek God's guidance when making every important decision.
3. It doesn't matter so much what I believe as long as I live a moral life.

4. In my life, I experience the presence of the Divine.
5. My faith sometimes restricts my actions.
6. Although I am a religious person, I refuse to let religious considerations influence my everyday affairs.
7. Nothing is as important to me as serving God as best I know how.
8. Although I believe in my religion, I feel there are many more important things in life.
9. I try hard to carry my religion over into all my other dealings in life.
10. My religious beliefs are what really lie behind my whole approach to life.

Narrative Faith Relevance Scale (Lee, 2004)

1. It is important to me that my future career somehow embody a calling from God.
2. I try to see setbacks and crises as part of God's larger plan.
3. If and when I date someone, it is (or would be) important to me that God be pleased with the relationship.
4. In thinking about my schedule, I try to cultivate the attitude that my time belongs to God.
5. It is important to me that whatever money I have be used to serve God's purposes.
6. In choosing what college to attend, it is important to me to seek God's will.
7. When I think of the things I own or would like to own, I try to remember that everything I have belongs to God.

Faith Maturity Scale (Benson et al, 1993)

1. I experience a deep communion with God.
2. My faith shapes how I think and act each and every day.

3. I help others with their religious questions and struggles.
4. My faith helps me know right from wrong.
5. I devote time to reading and studying the Bible.
6. Every day I see evidence that God is active in the world.
7. I seek out opportunities to help me grow spiritually.
8. I take time for periods of prayer or meditation.
9. I feel God's presence in my relationships with other people.
10. My life is filled with meaning and purpose.
11. I try to apply my faith to political and social issues.
12. My life is committed to Jesus Christ.
13. I go out of my way to show love to people I meet.
14. I have a real sense that God is guiding me.
15. I like to worship and pray with others.
16. I think Christians must be about the business of creating international understanding and harmony.
17. I am spiritually moved by the beauty of God's creation.

Religious Support Scale (Fiala et al, 2002)

1. God gives me the sense that I belong.
2. I feel appreciated by God.
3. If something went wrong, God would give me help.
4. I am valued by God.
5. I can turn to God for advice when I have problems.
6. God cares about my life and situation.
7. I do NOT feel close to God.

High School Version of Religious Behavior Scale (created for the CTP pilot)
For the following 8 items, please tell us how often you engaged in each of the behaviors listed, during *the past 12 months:* Less than once a month, About once a month, Two to three times a month, About once a week, Two to three times a week, Daily.

How often did you . . .

1. talk with another Christian about your faith, outside of a church-related context?
2. pray alone?
3. attend a worship service or church-related event?
4. speak or try to speak with a non-Christian about your faith?
5. volunteer your time to serve others?
6. participate in a small group of your peers for religious or spiritual purposes?
7. read your Bible by yourself?
8. meet with a spiritual mentor (other than your parents)?

College Version of Religious Behavior Scale

How often did you . . .

1. talk with another Christian about your faith, outside of a church-related context?
2. participate in an on-campus Christian fellowship?
3. pray alone?
4. attend a worship service or other event at a church off-campus?
5. speak or try to speak with a non-Christian about your faith?
6. volunteer your time to serve others?
7. participate in a small group of your peers for religious or spiritual purposes?
8. read your Bible by yourself?
9. attend a school-sponsored chapel?
10. meet with an older Christian for spiritual growth, mentoring, or discipleship?
11. participate in service or justice work that helps people in need?

notes

Chapter 1: The Not-So-Sticky Faith Reality

1. When we use the phrase "falling away" from the faith, we don't necessarily mean students have "lost" their salvation, but rather they have "fallen away" from a faith that places Jesus at the center of all they are and do.

2. Laurie Goodstein, "Evangelicals Fear the Loss of Their Teenagers," *The New York Times*, October 6, 2006.

3. In September 2006, the Barna Group released their observation that "the most potent data regarding disengagement is that a majority of twentysome-things—61 percent of today's young adults—had been churched at one point during their teen years but they are now spiritually disengaged" (Barna Update, "Most Twentysomethings Put Christianity on the Shelf Following Spiritually Active Teen Years," *The Barna Group,* September 16, 2006). According to a Gallup Poll, approximately 40 percent of eighteen- to twenty-nine-year-olds who attended church at age sixteen or seventeen are no longer attending (George H. Gallup, Jr. "The Religiosity Cycle," *The Gallup Poll,* June 4, 2002. Frank Newport, "A Look at Religious Switching in America Today," *The Gallup Poll,* June 23, 2006.

A 2007 survey by LifeWay Research of over one thousand adults ages eighteen to thirty who spent a year or more in youth group during high school suggests that more than 65 percent of young adults who attend a Protestant church for at least a year in high school will stop attending church regularly for at least a year between the ages of eighteen and twenty-two. (LifeWay, "LifeWay Research Uncovers Reasons 18 to 22 Year Olds Drop Out of Church," LifeWay Christian Resources, http://www.lifeway.com/article/165949/). In this study, respondents were not necessarily those who had graduated from youth group as seniors. In addition, the research design did not factor in parachurch or on-campus faith communities in their definition of college "church" attendance.

Data from the National Study of Youth and Religion published in 2009 indicate an approximate 30 percent drop in weekly or more frequent religious service attendance across multiple Protestant denominations. (Christian Smith and Patricia Snell, *Souls in Transition: The Religious & Spiritual Lives of Emerging Adults* [New York: Oxford University Press, 2009].)

Fuller Youth Insititute's estimate that 40 to 50 percent of high school graduates will fail to stick with their faith is based on a compilation of data from these various studies.

4. Quite a while after we started using the term *Sticky Faith* in our writing and seminars, we learned that there was a book by Group Publishing entitled *Sticky Faith*. A year later, we read the term *sticky faith* in Diana Garland's *Inside Out Families*. While we came up with the term *Sticky Faith* independently, we are glad other thoughtful leaders are devoting energy to helping kids' and families' faith stick.

5. "LifeWay Research Uncovers Reasons 18 to 22 Year Olds Drop Out of Church," http://www.lifeway.com/article/165949/.

6. The percentage varies greatly by denomination; conservative Protestants are more likely to return than Roman Catholics or mainline Protestants (Wade Clark Roof and Lyn Gesch, "Boomers and the Culture of Choice: Changing Patterns of Work, Family and Religion," *Work, Family, and Religion in Contemporary Society,* ed. Nancy Tatom Ammerman and Wade Clark Roof [New York: Routledge, 1995], 61–79).

7. The National Center on Addiction and Substance Abuse at Columbia University, "Wasting the Best and the Brightest: Substance Abuse at America's Colleges and Universities," March 2007, i.

8. Henry Wechsler and Bernice Wuethrich, *Dying to Drink: Confronting Binge Drinking on College Campuses* (Emmaus, PA: Rodale 2002), 4, 21.

9. Wechsler and Wuethrich, *Dying to Drink,* 4, 28.

10. Michael Kimmel, *Guyland* (New York: Harper Collins, 2008), 199.

11. Kimmel, *Guyland,* 195.

12. Kimmel, *Guyland,* 58.

13. Carolyn McNamara Barry and Larry J. Nelson, "The Role of Religion in the Transition to Adulthood for Young Emerging Adults," *Journal of Youth and Adolescence* 34, no. 3 (2005): 245–55; Patrick L. Dulin, Robert D. Hill, and Kari Ellingson, "Relationships among Religious Factors, Social Support and Alcohol Abuse in a Western U.S. College Student Sample," *Journal of Alcohol and Drug Education* 50, no. 1 (2004): 5–14; Eva S. Lefkowitz, Meghan M. Gillen, Cindy L. Shearer, and Tanya L. Boone, "Religiosity, Sexual Behaviors, and Sexual Attitudes during Emerging Adulthood," *The Journal of Sex Research* 41, no. 2 (2004): 150–59; Melissa S. Strawser, Eric A. Storch, Gary R. Geffken, Erin M. Killiany, and Audrey L. Baumeister, "Religious Faith and Substance Problems in Undergraduate College Students: A Replication," *Pastoral Psychology* 53, no. 2 (2004): 183–88.

14. The College Transition Project is comprised of four separate research initiatives: An initial quantitative pilot study involving 69 youth group graduates; two three-year longitudinal (primarily quantitative) studies of high school seniors during their first three years in college, involving 162 and 227 students respectively; and additional qualitative interviews with 45 former youth group graduates who are currently in college. For more on our research methodology, see the Appendix and visit www.stickyfaith.org.

15. LifeWay Research Uncovers Reasons 18 to 22 Year Olds Drop Out of Church," http://www.lifeway.com/article/165949/.

16. We wrestled with how to describe the fact that God cares about and interacts with each individual and yet much of our faith growth is communal. *Personal* is our best attempt—but in using that term, we do not mean to imply an individualistic faith.

17. Because of these three characteristics, we quantified Sticky Faith through a compilation of valid and reliable faith maturity scales that focus on internalized paradigms and beliefs, motivation for those values and beliefs, and more "externalized" behaviors (both public and private faith practices like prayer, service, and church attendance). In addition, at times we also looked at involvement in a church or parachurch ministry as a further sign of Sticky Faith.

18. Our research was designed to reveal factors in students, their families, their youth ministries, and their churches that were related with Sticky Faith. Please note our research was not designed to prove causation but to discover strong correlations between variables that might predict the relationships between those variables.

19. Tim Clydesdale, *The First Year Out* (Chicago: University of Chicago Press, 2007), 205.

Chapter 2: The Sticky Gospel

1. Krista M. Kubiak Crotty, *Spirituality, religiosity, and risk behaviors in high school seniors transitioning to college* (Psy.D. dissertation, Azusa Pacific University, 2009).

2. Part of that data can be explained by what statisticians call "regression to the mean," which means that those who didn't drink or have sex at all have nowhere to go but up. But as we have talked extensively with college students, we have seen that it's more than that.

3. Dallas Willard, *The Divine Conspiracy* (New York: HarperCollins, 1998), 41.

4. A special thank-you to our good friend and colleague, Chap Clark, for collaborating on this chapter, especially the analysis of Galatians 5:1-6.

5. Male circumcision is the removal of some, or all, of the foreskin of the penis. The history of circumcision dates back to the opening chapters of Scripture. In Genesis 17, God initiated a covenant with Abraham, the patriarch of the Hebrews; Abraham's part of the covenant included: "Every male among you shall be circumcised" (v. 10).

6. Leaning on the Old Testament that affirms God's intent behind the ritual, Paul establishes the importance of a "circumcision of the heart" as described in Jeremiah 4:4. In Christ, the outward rite was replaced with an inward rebirth, and while Paul never teaches that physical circumcision was categorically wrong, in other epistles Paul clarifies that it is no longer a requirement: "Circumcision is nothing and uncircumcision is nothing" (1 Corinthians 7:19). Paul's point is that when we think we can somehow achieve perfection and holiness by relying on any external ritual or rite, we deny the reason for the gospel.

7. *The New Testament in Modern English*, J. B. Phillips (London: G. Bles, 1958). For more biblical explanation of this, see Romans 8, especially 8:2-4.

8. Michael Horton, "Union with Christ," 1992, http://www.monergism.com/thethreshold/articles/questions/horton/union.html.

9. Thanks to Meredith Miller for her collaboration on implications for teaching kids the Sticky Gospel.

Chapter 3: Sticky Identity

1. In particular, there is much research demonstrating a link between genetics and personality factors, or predispositions to certain behaviors and tendencies, such as aggression and nurturing. See V. Elving Anderson, "A Genetic View of Human Nature," in *Whatever Happened to the Soul?* eds. Warren S. Brown, Nancey Murphy, and H. Newton Malony (Minneapolis: Fortress Press, 1998), 49–72.

2. See Erik H. Erikson, *Identity and the Life Cycle* (New York: W. W. Norton & Co., 1959, 1980).

3. Chap Clark, *Hurt 2.0: Inside the World of Today's Teenagers.* (Grand Rapids: Baker Academic, 2011; original edition 2004). After observing and interviewing students in Virginia, Patricia Hersch describes the same phenomenon in *A Tribe Apart: A Journey into the Heart of American Adolescence.* (New York: Ballantine, 1998).

4. Developmentalist Robert Kegan has proposed another stage to Erikson's psychosocial theory, inserting it prior to adolescence. Basically, it is intended to cover the junior high years, ages 11 to 13. He calls this stage Affiliation vs. Abandonment, and he describes the dilemma as a highly motivated drive toward affiliation and belonging, in fear of being abandoned and left behind by friends. Our college freshmen express the same drive and need—going to all lengths to make sure they are included and not abandoned. For more detail, see Robert Kegan, *The Evolving Self: Problem and Process in Human Development* (Cambridge: Harvard University Press, 1982).

5. Most college freshmen who commute from home to college continue their high school patterns of behavior, with the same group of high school friends.

6. Whereas Erikson would describe someone who isn't interested or able to grapple with his or her identity as "role-confused," Marcia uses the term "diffused" to describe an adolescent who simply hasn't engaged the identity process yet. Erikson sees this as a task that must be accomplished in order to successfully continue through his other stages, whereas Marcia sees "diffused" as a temporary state during the identity process.

7. James E. Marcia, "Development and Validation of Ego Identity Status," *Journal of Personality and Social Psychology* 3 (1966): 551–558. Also James E. Marcia, "Identity in Adolescence," in *Handbook of Adolescent Psychology,* ed. Joseph Adelson (New York: John Wiley & Sons, 1980).

8. See Tim Clydesdale, *The First Year Out* (Chicago: The University of Chicago Press, 2007).

9. The foundational Nouwen books explaining these thoughts are *In the Name of Jesus* (New York: Crossroad, 1989) and *Life of the Beloved* (New York: Crossroad, 1992).

10. Nouwen, *Life of the Beloved,* 30.

11. J. J. Arnett defines emerging adulthood as a socially constructed period between ages 18 and 27, characterized by *identity explorations, instability,*

self-focus, an *in-between feeling,* and a *sense of great possibilities.* For detailed descriptions of each of these characteristics, see J. J. Arnett, *Emerging Adulthood: The Winding Road from the Late Teens through the Twenties* (New York: Oxford University Press, 2004).

12. See Eugene C. Roehlkepartain and Eboo Patel, "Congregations: Unexamined Crucibles for Spiritual Development," in *The Handbook of Spiritual Development in Childhood and Adolesence,* eds. E. C. Roehlkepartain, P. E. King, L. M. Wagener, and P. L. Benson (Thousand Oaks, CA: Sage, 2006), 324.

13. Will Willimon, "Ritual and Pastoral Care," in *The Conviction of Things Not Seen: Worship and Ministry in the 21st Century,* ed. Todd Johnson (Grand Rapids: Brazos Press, 2002), 100–101. Willimon further notes that "The presence of much ritual at some human gatherings is not necessarily a testimonial to our dull, habituated tendencies, but rather, attests to the challenge of the difficult life transition that is being negotiated at the gathering" (p. 102).

14, Nathan Mitchell, *Liturgy and the Social Sciences* (Collegeville, MN: The Liturgical Press, 1999), 42. By nature, then, rituals are dangerous because we are hoping that a somewhat artificial practice will communicate a very real, deep truth. Ritual is always fully embodied in culture and history, never timeless or "generic." In this sense, the rewriting of ritual is necessary to communicate meaning in our unique contexts.

15. These are elements from a service found in the hymnal *This Far by Faith: An African American Resource for Worship* (Minneapolis: Augsburg Fortress, 1999), 105.

16. Peter C. Scales, Eugene C. Roehlkepartain, and Peter L. Benson, *Teen Voice 2010: Relationships That Matter to America's Teens* (Minneapolis and Richfield, MN: Search Institute and Best Buy Children's Foundation, 2010).

17. See Gay Holcomb and Arthur Nonneman, "Faithful Change: Exploring and Assessing Faith Development in Christian Liberal Arts Undergraduates," in *Assessing Character Outcomes in College: New Directions for Institutional Research No. 122,* eds. Dalton et al (San Francisco: Jossey-Bass, 2004), 93–103.

18.Margaret Hall, "Crisis as Opportunity for Spiritual Growth," *Journal of Religion and Health* 25, no. 1 (Spring 1986): 8–17.

Chapter 4: Sticky Churches

1. Judith Gundry-Volf, "To Such as These Belongs the Reign of God," *Theology Today* 56(4), (2000): 475–476.

2. Adapted from a November 2008 *FYI E-Journal* article by David Fraze entitled "Theological Principles Behind Intergenerational Youth Ministry: It's Not Rocket Science," available at www.fulleryouthinstitute.org.

3. Our FYI research finding about the importance of serving at church parallels previous examinations of students' transition from high school to college. In Carol Lytch's in-depth ethnographic study of three diverse churches, she noted an "opportunity to develop competence" as one of three factors that consistently attracted and kept high school students at church (Carol Lytch, *Choosing Church: What Makes a Difference for Teens* (Louisville: Westminster John Knox, 2004), 39ff). In addition, the LifeWay Research study of 1,000 adults ages

18 to 30 found that having regular responsibilities of the church during high school was one of the church activities that was most closely correlated with maintaining church involvement after graduation. ("LifeWay Research Uncovers Reasons 18 to 22 Year Olds Drop Out of Church," http://www.lifeway.com/article/165949/.

4. "LifeWay Research Uncovers Reasons 18 to 22 Year Olds Drop Out of Church," http://www.lifeway.com/article/165949/.

5. Adapted from Kara Powell, *Essential Leadership* (Grand Rapids: Youth Specialties/Zondervan, 2010), 78–79.

6. Erika C. Knuth, *Intergenerational Connections and Faith Development in Late Adolescence,* Unpublished Doctoral Dissertation (Pasadena, CA: Fuller Theological Seminary, Graduate School of Psychology, 2010).

7. Reggie Joiner, Chuck Bomar, and Abbie Smith, *The Slow Fade* (Colorado Springs: David C. Cook, 2010), 63.

8. David Fraze, "A Church in the Intergenerational HOV Lane," *FYI E-Journal,* February 2, 2009, http://fulleryouthinstitute.org/2009/02/a-church-in-the-intergenerational-hov-lane/.

9. Stanley Hauerwas, Carole Bailey Stoneking, Keith G. Meador, and David Cloutier, *Growing Old in Christ* (Grand Rapids: Eerdmans, 2003), 182.

Chapter 5: Sticky Justice

1. David A. Livermore, *Cultural Intelligence: Improving Your CQ to Engage Our Multicultural World* (Grand Rapids: Baker Academic, 2009), 26.

2. Kurt Ver Beek, "The Impact of Short-Term Missions: A Case Study of House Construction in Honduras after Hurricane Mitch," *Missiology* 34, no. 4 (October 2006): 485.

3. Nicholas Wolterstorff, "The Contours of Justice: An Ancient Call for Shalom," in *God and the Victim: Theological Reflections on Evil, Victimization, Justice, and Forgiveness,* eds. Lisa Barnes Lampman and Michelle D. Shattuck (Grand Rapids: Eerdmans, 1999), 113.

4. Tim Arango, "Make Room, Cynics; MTV Wants to Do Some Good," *New York Times,* April 18, 2009, http://www.nytimes.com/2009/04/19/business/media/19mtv.html.

5. Eugene C. Roehlkepartain, Elanah Dalyah Naftali, and Laura Musegades, *Growing Up Generous: Engaging Youth in Giving and Serving* (Bethesda, MD: Alban Institute, 2000), 116.

6. Robert J. Priest, Terry Dischinger, Steve Rasmussen, C. M. Brown, "Researching the Short-Term Mission Movement," *Missiology* 34, no. 4 (October 2006): 431–450.

7. MTV's national survey was comprised of 1,308 12- to 24-year-olds who completed online surveys and 98 students who were interviewed personally.

8. This research can be accessed at http://www.mtv.com/thinkmtv/research/.

9. We are deeply indebted to our co-researchers Dave Livermore and Terry Linhart for the design and facilitation of these summits, in addition to all of the participants who sacrificially gave their time and deep insights: Jared Ayers, George Bache, Noel Becchetti, Terry Bley, Todd Bratulich, Tom Carpenter, Sean

Cooper, April Diaz, Brian Dietz, Joel Fay, Hal Hamilton, Brian Heerwagen, Eric Iverson, Tom Ives, Cari Jenkins, Johnny Johnston, Kent Koteskey, Sandy Liu, Mark Maines, Mark Matlock, Daryl Nuss, Derry Prenkert, Kurt Rietema, David Russell, David Schultz, Rich Van Pelt, Bob Whittet, and Kimberly Williams.

10. The following section is adapted from an article coauthored by Kara Powell, Dave Livermore, Terry Linhart, and Brad Griffin entitled "If We Send Them, They Will Grow . . . Maybe," available at www.fulleryouthinstitute.org.

11. Laura Joplin, "On Defining Experiential Education" in *The Theory of Experiential Education*, eds. K. Warren, M. Sakofs, and J. S. Hunt Jr. (Dubuque, IA: Kendall/Hunt Publishing Company, 1995), 15–22.

12. Terrence D. Linhart, "Planting Seeds: The Curricular Hope of Short Term Mission Experiences in Youth Ministry," *Christian Education Journal*, Series 3, (2005), 256–272. Some of the terminology in the model has been modified.

13. This model is fully explained in Kara Powell and Brad Griffin, *Deep Justice Journeys* (Grand Rapids: Youth Specialties/Zondervan, 2009). In *Deep Justice Journeys*, 50 Before/During/After learning activities are provided to help your students move from mission trips to missional living.

14. Sara Corbett, "A Prom Divided," *The New York Times*, May 21, 2009. http://www.nytimes.com/2009/05/24/magazine/24prom-t.html.

Chapter 6: Sticky Family Relationships

1. Christian Smith with Melinda Lundquist Denton, *Soul Searching: The Religious and Spiritual Lives of American Teenagers* (New York: Oxford Press, 2005), 56.

2. Listen to the "Soul Searching" panel discussion from March 2008 at the FYI website: http://fulleryouthinstitute.org/2008/03/soul-searching-panel/.

3. Search Institute research report, *Effective Christian Education: A National Study of Protestant Congregations*, 1990.

4. One study of 4,000 Christian adolescents indicates that both parents' modeling of faith and their conversations about faith were related to higher faith among their children. Kelly D. Schwartz, "Transformations in Parent and Friend Faith Support Predicting Adolescents' Religious Faith," *The International Journal for the Psychology of Religion* 16, no. 4 (2006), 311–326.

5. Those two data sets are the National Study of Youth and Religion and the National Longitudinal Study of Adolescent Health. Mark D. Regnerus, *Forbidden Fruit* (New York: Oxford University Press, 2007), 60-73.

6. Dallas Willard, *The Divine Conspiracy* (San Francisco: Harper Collins, 1998), 40.

7. Reggie Joiner and Carey Nieuwhof, *Parenting Beyond Your Capacity* (Colorado Springs: David C. Cook Publishing, 2010), 69–70.

8. Max De Pree, *Leadership Is an Art* (New York: Doubleday, 1989), 9.

Chapter 7: Sticky Youth Groups

1. Dustin Junkert, "What My Faith in God Looks Like," *New York Times*, July 20, 2009, http://www.nytimes.com/2009/07/26/education/edlife/26god.html).

2. Erika C. Knuth, *Intergenerational Connections and Faith Development in Late*

Adolescence, Unpublished Doctoral Dissertation (Pasadena, CA: Fuller Theological Seminary, Graduate School of Psychology, 2010).

3. Note that these weren't just what students chose as most important to them, but what seemed to have the strongest connection to the faith variables in our survey. Erika C. Knuth, *Intergenerational Connections and Faith Development in Late Adolescence.*

4. This lack of personal spiritual practice can be damaging to Sticky Faith. Christian Smith's research through the National Study of Youth and Religion found that one factor in predicting stronger young adult faith is teenagers who have "established devotional lives—that is, praying, reading Scripture—during the teenage years. Those who do so as teenagers are much more likely than those who don't to continue doing so into emerging adulthood." See "Lost in Transition," an interview with Christian Smith by Katelyn Beaty, *Christianity Today,* Oct 9, 2009, http://www.christianitytoday.com/ct/2009/october/21.34.html. Also see Christian Smith and Patricia Snell, *Souls in Transition: The Religious and Spiritual Lives of Emerging Adults* (Oxford University Press, 2009).

5. Derek Melleby, "Life After High School: The First Year," http://www.cpyu.org/Page.aspx?id=387650.

6. See the following books from Mark Yaconelli: *Downtime: Helping Teenagers Pray* (Grand Rapids: Youth Specialties/Zondervan, 2008); *Growing Souls: Experiments in Contemplative Youth Ministry* (Grand Rapids: Youth Specialties/Zondervan, 2007); and *Contemplative Youth Ministry: Practicing the Presence of Jesus* (Grand Rapids: Youth Specialties/Zondervan, 2006). Practices such as the *examen* and *lectio divina,* among many others, are detailed in *Downtime* and *Contemplative Youth Ministry.*

7. Robert Kegan, *In Over Our Heads: The Mental Demands of Modern Life* (Cambridge: Harvard University Press, 1994), 42.

8. Thomas Bergler and Dave Rahn, "Results of a Collaborative Research Project in Gathering Evangelism Stories," *Journal of Youth Ministry* 4, no. 2 (Spring 2006): 65–74.

9. For a thoughtful and stirring take on ministry relationships, see Andy Root's *Revisiting Relational Youth Ministry: From a Strategy of Influence to a Theology of Incarnation* (Downers Grove, IL: InterVarsity Press, 2007). Root's basic thesis is that we've long viewed relationships as strategies to gain influence in kids' lives (influence that will hopefully lead them to Jesus). This is perhaps misreading the theological grounds of the incarnation, which instead views the relationship itself as the place where Christ is present. Root argues for a ministry of "place sharing" rather than "strategic influence."

10. Note: While we support speaking of Christian community as "family," in doing so we do not intend to devalue the importance of the biological/adoptive nuclear family or minimize the influence of parents and siblings on a teenager's life. We think that comes out in chapter 6, but we just wanted to say it again to be clear.

11. See Carol Lytch, *Choosing Church* (Louisville: John Knox Press, 2004). Based on in-depth ethnographic research of adolescents in their youth groups and congregations, Lytch discovered that building competence through

leadership or service of some sort was one of the factors connected with the choice to stick with church—and faith.

Chapter 8: Sticky Seniors

1. As we mentioned in chapter 3 ("Sticky Identity"), sociologist Tim Clydesdale also found that freshmen become all-consumed with the game he calls "daily life management." Facing the sudden instability of their new environment, schedule, and virtually limitless boundaries, operating from day to day becomes a practice of sheer survival. Clydesdale describes college students' new juggling act this way: "[T]hey manage their personal relationships—with romantic partners, friends, and authority figures; they manage personal gratifications—including substance use and sexual activity; and they manage their economic lives—with its expanding necessities and rising lifestyle expectations." Tim Clydesdale, *The First Year Out* (Chicago: University of Chicago Press, 2007), 2, also see 73–74.

2. According to Kathy Chu, "College Students Using Plastic More," *USA Today,* April 13, 2009, and "Credit Card Statistics, Industry Facts, Debt Statistics," http://www.creditcards.com/credit-card-news/credit-card-industry-facts-personal-debt-statistics-1276.php.

3. The seminal work on this theory can be found in Arnold Van Gennep, *The Rites of Passage,* trans. Monika B. Vizedom and Garielle L. Caffee (Chicago: University of Chicago Press, 1960 [orig. 1908]), and Victor Turner and Edith L. B. Turner, *Image and Pilgrimage in Christian Culture: Anthropological Perspectives* (New York: Columbia University Press, 1978).

4. Kenneth R. Mitchell and Herbert Anderson, *All Our Losses, All Our Griefs: Resources for Pastoral Care* (Louisville, KY: Westminster John Knox Press, 1983) 36–46.

Chapter 9: The Path to Sticky Change

1. Scott Cormode, Sticky Faith Summit, February 2010, Pasadena, CA.

2. Ronald A. Heifetz, *Leadership Without Easy Answers* (Cambridge: Belknap/Harvard University Press, 1994).

3. Adapted from William Ury, *Getting Past NO: Negotiating Your Way from Confrontation to Cooperation* (New York: Bantam, 1991).

4. Scott Cormode, "Action Plan Questions," a handout prepared for the Sticky Faith Learning Cohort, March 2010.

5. John P. Kotter, "Leading Change: Why Transformation Efforts Fail," *Harvard Business Review,* March-April 1995.

6. Kotter, "Leading Change."

Appendix: The College Transition Project: Research Overview

1. Xianglei Chen, Joanna Wu, Shayna Tasoff, "The High School Senior Class of 2003–04: Steps Toward Postsecondary Enrollment," U.S. Department of Education, National Center for Education Statistics, February 2010, table 4, http://nces.ed.gov/pubs2010/2010203.pdf.

2. D. R. Hoge, "A Validated Intrinsic Religious Motivation Scale," *Journal for the Scientific Study of Religion* 11 (1972): 369–76.

3. Cameron Lee, "Narrative Faith Relevance Scale" (unpublished manuscript, 2004).

4. P. L. Benson, M. J. Donahue, and J. A. Erickson, "The Faith Maturity Scale: Conceptualization, Measurement, and Empirical Validation," *Research in the Social Scientific Study of Religion* 5 (1993): 1–26.

5. William E. Fiala, Jeffrey P. Bjorck, and Richard Gorsuch, "The Religious Support Scale: Construction, Validation, and Cross-Validation," *American Journal of Community Psychology* 30 (2002): 761–86.

Sticky Faith Curriculum for Teenagers with DVD

10 Lessons to Nurture Faith beyond High School

Kara E. Powell and Brad M. Griffin

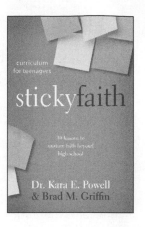

Churches are waking up to the reality that almost half of their high school students struggle deeply with their faith in college. Offering special high school "Senior Seminars" or giving seniors a graduation Bible and hoping for the best are too little, too late.

In response to this problem, the Fuller Youth Institute conducted a national study to answer the question: What can youth workers do to help students develop a lasting faith in God? By following high school seniors into their first three years of college to gain an understanding of the transition from high school to college, they found their answers. And *Sticky Faith Curriculum for Teenagers* enables youth leaders to impact to their students with a faith that sticks.

This 10-session book and DVD study gives youth workers a theological and philosophical framework alongside real-world, road-tested programming ideas. The study is designed to help high school students develop a solid foundation that endures through the faith struggles they will face in college. Learn more at *www.stickyfaith.org*.

Available in stores and online!

ZONDERVAN®
.com

Sticky Faith

Everyday Ideas to Build Lasting Faith in Your Kids

Kara E. Powell and Chap Clark

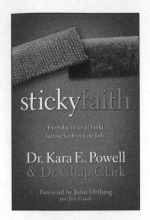

Nearly every Christian parent in America would give anything to find a viable resource for developing within their kids a deep, dynamic faith that "sticks" long term.

Sticky Faith delivers.

Research shows that almost half of graduating high school seniors struggle deeply with their faith. Recognizing the ramifications of that statistic, the Fuller Youth Institute (FYI) conducted the "College Transition Project" in an effort to identify the relationships and best practices that can set young people on a trajectory of lifelong faith and service.

Based on FYI findings, this easy-to-read guide presents both a compelling rationale and a powerful strategy to show parents how to actively encourage their children's spiritual growth so that it will stick to them into adulthood and empower them to develop a living, lasting faith.

Written by authors known for the integrity of their research and the intensity of their passion for young people, Sticky Faith is geared to spark a movement that empowers adults to develop robust and long-term faith in kids of all ages. Learn more at *www.stickyfaith.org*.

Available in stores and online!

Sticky Faith Parent Curriculum DVD

Everyday Ideas to Build Lasting Faith in Your Kids

Kara E. Powell

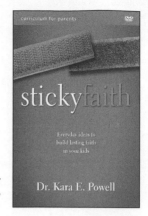

Most parents would give anything to anchor their children with a vibrant faith that "sticks" and continues to mature into adulthood. Yet, despite this deep desire, research indicates that approximately 40-50 percent of high school seniors drift from their faith after graduation.

The *Sticky Faith Parent Curriculum* is a video-based study that came from Kara Powell's desire to see her own kids emerge from adolescence with their faith intact. Through personal, real-world experiences of research and sharing, the *Sticky Faith Parent Curriculum* enables parents to instill a deep and lasting faith in their adolescents.

This video curriculum presents powerful strategies and practical ideas to help parents encourage their children's spiritual growth, enabling them to develop a faith that sticks. Learn more at *www.stickyfaith.org.*

Available in stores and online!

Share Your Thoughts

With the Author: Your comments will be forwarded to the author when you send them to *zauthor@zondervan.com*.

With Zondervan: Submit your review of this book by writing to *zreview@zondervan.com*.

Free Online Resources at
www.zondervan.com

Zondervan AuthorTracker: Be notified whenever your favorite authors publish new books, go on tour, or post an update about what's happening in their lives at www.zondervan.com/authortracker.

Daily Bible Verses and Devotions: Enrich your life with daily Bible verses or devotions that help you start every morning focused on God. Visit www.zondervan.com/newsletters.

Free Email Publications: Sign up for newsletters on Christian living, academic resources, church ministry, fiction, children's resources, and more. Visit www.zondervan.com/newsletters.

Zondervan Bible Search: Find and compare Bible passages in a variety of translations at www.zondervanbiblesearch.com.

Other Benefits: Register to receive online benefits like coupons and special offers, or to participate in research.

ZONDERVAN®

ZONDERVAN.com/
AUTHORTRACKER
follow your favorite authors